SO YOU WANT TO WORK FROM HOME WITHOUT LEAVING YOUR CURRENT JOB

• Business Essentials for Working Remotely •

FRANCES D. SZABO

iUniverse, Inc.
Bloomington

So You Want to Work from Home without Leaving Your Current Job
Business Essentials for Working Remotely

iUniverse books may be ordered through booksellers or by contacting:

iUniverse
1663 Liberty Drive
Bloomington, IN 47403
www.iuniverse.com
1-800-Authors (1-800-288-4677)

ISBN: 978-1-4502-6234-7 (sc)
ISBN: 978-1-4502-6235-4 (hc)
ISBN: 978-1-4502-6236-1 (ebk)

Library of Congress Control Number: 2010915435

Printed in the United States of America

iUniverse rev. date: 11/10/2010

To all my colleagues, who have offered their tips and techniques about working at home without leaving their jobs.

A special thank you to Karen A. Vollmer, the best editor I know!

Epigraph

One's philosophy is not best expressed in words; it's expressed in the choices one makes. In the long run, we shape our lives, and we shape ourselves. The process never stops until we die. And the choices we make are ultimately our responsibility.
—Eleanor Roosevelt

Contents

Foreword

When Fran told me about writing this book, I thought, "Who better to provide guidance on how an employee can work at home efficiently?" She was my manager for several years, and she had the insight to see that I was always stressed out by the commute, driving in inclement weather, and constant interruptions while in the office during the day.

Fran asked me if her observations were correct, and I confirmed them. She told me that she did not want to lose me as an employee, and I loved my job—other than the stress, worries and constant interruptions—so we discussed some alternatives.

We assessed the responsibilities of my job and concluded that twenty-four hours of my job each week could be accomplished from home. So we created a schedule for me to work at home three days a week and in the office two days a week. Fran made sure I understood that there might be weeks when that schedule would not be possible, depending on the company's business issues. The stress I had been feeling eased, knowing that I could telecommute some of the time.

Fran and I met later that day to review some tips and techniques for working at home. First, she told me that working at home was not for everyone. Some people find home to be more distracting than the office. Some people miss the daily socializing in the office and find it difficult to work alone. She also gave me some advice to help me succeed at working from home.

She shared so much that I had to take notes. She told me not to expect that all of her tips would work for me and not to be frustrated if it took a little time to find my groove. The following are just a few of the tips she shared, but there are many more in this book:

- Designate a space in your home in which to work.
- Learn to be a virtual team member.
- Use e-communication effectively.
- Practice stress-relieving techniques when you get frustrated.
- Prioritize your day/week.
- Take breaks.
- Create time boundaries.
- Laugh.

We agreed to a thirty-day trial to see if the new schedule would work for me and for the company. If it did work, there would be a small investment, at my expense, to implement a few more of the tips she shared. It worked! I made the investment of three hundred dollars and became even more productive.

Soon after my new schedule was working well, some of the other employees became jealous and thought it was not fair that I could work from home three days a week and others could not. Fran explained to them that many job responsibilities cannot be done outside of the office. She met with those employees as she had with me. Some employees worked out alternative schedules, and it was not possible for others.

Fran is a great leader and mentor. She helped me and allowed me to find better balance in my life and to become an even more valuable contributor to the company. I know by reading this book that "Dr. Fran" can help.

I asked Fran how she accomplishes so much and still keeps it together.

"I work from home as often as I can," she said.

Maria Chavez
Executive Assistant, Marriott International, Bethesda, Maryland

Preface

My inspiration for this book was twofold. The first was my strong sense of empathy and concern for the well-being and success of those individuals who supported me in the corporate offices of well-known Fortune 100 companies. The second inspirational nugget is of a slightly more selfish nature, but it's sincerely truthful—working from home preserved my sanity. Moreover, two previous managers, Sandy Shaw and Randy Harris, helped nurture my pro–alternative-work-arrangement spirit, because they also understood the relevance of these concepts and mentored me to be productive and in control of my surroundings.

Most employees don't come to work every day wondering how they can make it a horrible or difficult day. Not only do most people want to be successful in their daily endeavors, but I also believe that most people feel a certain type of positive energy when they have some control over their work environments. This is a reward that an employee can reap by working from a home office. The percentage of employees who reported that their jobs were very or extremely stressful has doubled in a decade (from 40 percent in 1994 to 80 percent in 2001).

Despite rapid advances in technology that allow people to conduct international business, commonly from a small work space in a corporate building, only a small percentage of employees in jobs suitable for working remotely (from home) are actually working from home. It does take discipline to work under the same roof in which you live. However, I have learned through my own personal experience and through the experiences of others that, if you can do it right, working remotely from your own home office can be highly rewarding. And you can keep your job, too.

Some people find that there are a hundred things to do around the house before they begin their work for pay. Some find the seclusion depressing, which can greatly affect their productivity; they miss the daily socializing that naturally occurs in an office. Others do not have the space or equipment in their homes to create an effective, efficient, and productive home office.

Establishing a functional routine is critical. It's important to keep your office work routine, as if you are commuting to the actual office site. Sometimes you have to modify your routine. For example, because my business is international, I work with people in various time zones, and I may need to have conference calls at 3:00 AM or 7:00 PM to accommodate another company's business schedule. Obviously, my routine is not so routine on those days; that is where flexibility becomes important. When I began working from home a couple days a week, I could adjust my schedule to accommodate the different time zones. This type of situation did not automatically translate into a very long work day.

My education taught me some of the ideas I have written about in this book. I hold a doctorate degree in business management from Revans University, a master's degree in human resources and organizational development from the University of San Francisco, and a bachelor's degree in psychology from the University of California, Davis. Despite the formal degrees I have received, I did not necessarily learn all the tips and techniques presented in this book from my formal education. I learned a great deal from fellow business owners who also work from their homes, including Tom Szabo (my brother), Robert L. Dilworth, Barbara Nouveau, and Cheryl Johnson. I have also added to their lessons through the School of Hard Knocks education, provided to me throughout my thirty-year career.

We all have our own habits, methods for motivation, and approaches to accomplishing work. If something works for you, your way is the right way—for you. I remember once being surprised to receive e-mail from an employee at 1:00 AM. It just did not fit my paradigm. After all, I'm a morning person but not that early. However, I shifted my paradigm by acknowledging and understanding that, for her, that particular time of day was very productive.

I also learned from other employees who successfully work from home: Karen Vollmer, Cindy Hummelbrunner, Noreen Felouzis, Laurent Ndeze, Lou Fiore, and Mary Beth Andres. I thank them for what they have shared with me about how they have made working from home truly work for them as well as for the people they support at the corporate offices. I have read many books and searched many Web sites that are recognized in this work. Although there are several books and articles published about working from home, I have not come across any that take the angle of making the alternative work schedule case for you.

So You Want to Work from Home without Leaving Your Current Job will provide:

- evidence that working from home can benefit both the employee and employer;
- techniques to make working from home successful;
- a platform from which a dialogue with the manager can convince him or her of the idea;
- tips to improve productivity and balance working from home; and
- some additional references.

Introduction

Twenty years ago, alternative work schedules were virtually unheard of and organizations in the private sector have been continually reinventing their businesses to improve profit, increase customer satisfaction, and reduce costs through people processes, business processes, sales and marketing. The manager of the past has become a shadow (Childress and Senn 1995).

Careers have changed in the past few decades. Many companies have chosen to shift some of their workloads to contract employees who either work at the company's office or work from their homes. This latter type of employee generally saves a company money, because the company can refrain from having to supply and pay rent on a space (a "cube" or office) and benefits for these individuals. In return, the employee (contractor) avoids the daily commute and can adjust his/her schedule to accomplish the work without ever leaving home.

Today, more and more companies are turning their traditional organizational charts upside down. Rather than the CEO at the top of the chart, companies are placing employees, who are actually closest to the work being done, at the top of the model (Buckingham and Coffman 1999). This contemporary model allows employees at all levels in the organization to understand that they influence the company's results. When employees are asked to improve the way the work they do gets done, productivity increases, which positively impacts the organization's results (Dilworth and Willis 2003).

According to Churchard (2009 Job cuts needn't harm employee performance. www.peoplemanagement.co.uk/pm/articles/2009/04/ job-cuts-neednt-harm-performance-argues-think-tank-chief.htm), companies increased their employee development efforts in 2008 by 22 percent in the hopes of improving employee retention and morale as well as to help offset the recessional effects that were beginning to make waves in companies nationwide. The organizations that find the resources to invest in employees, especially considering the current economic times, understand the power of employee morale.

A very simple and well-known theory identifies the link between employee morale and profitability (Heskett, Sasser, and Schlesinger 1997). It is referred to as the Service Profit Chain.

SERVICE PROFIT CHAIN

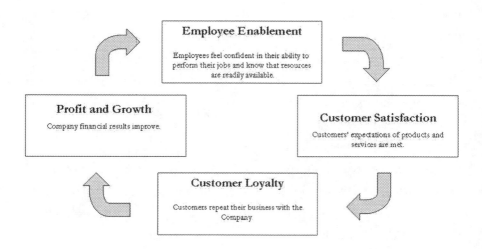

Employee enablement is comprised of many things. Employees need the tools, resources, training, teamwork, adequate working conditions,

respect, and control to perform their jobs successfully. Kaye and Jordan-Evans (2003) have found that the most important benefit—but least likely to be provided—to employees is control. Employees must be given room to initiate, create, and implement new ideas. They must be able to articulate the importance of their jobs to their managers and the overall organization that they support. Employees also thrive on new challenges and variety in their tasks and surroundings.

Most employees want to be busy and productive at work (Kaye 1997; Cottrell and Harvey 2005). They don't go to work wondering how they can make it a miserable day (Sanborn 2004). The difference between liking a job and loving a job is having control over the way work can be completed and where this is done (Kaye and Jordan-Evans 2003). Gallup (2009 Gallup conducts retention study, retrieved on line January 15, 2010 from www.Vovici.com) conducted a retention study and concluded that 47 percent of top-performing employees are actively looking for jobs outside of their present positions. The lack of control that employees can feel is not always due to the manager's style. It could be due to stress factors such as commuting, distractions in the workplace, or a rigid routine and daily schedule (Cottrell, Carnes, and Layton 2003).

Many jobs can be preformed successfully from home, part- or full-time. Obviously, some jobs must be conducted on the organization's premises. Working from home takes discipline, so it may not be the right fit for everyone.

Every day, more professionals are embracing working at home. Being close to the family, not having to commute, and creating your own schedule are wonderful ways to work and enjoy life at the same time. Should you choose to work from home, you must be very dedicated to producing a certain amount of work every day and preserving the work rules that you and your company make for yourself.

The Bureau of Labor Statistics (2007) estimates that 14 percent of employees in the private sector are in licensed, home-based businesses.

In a personal communication, Barbara Brown of the bureau estimated that another 10 percent of people work from their homes rather than at their employer's facilities, but it is difficult to track these statistics.

Your Situation

Even though you are working alone from your home, you can still be a virtual team player. In general, employees can be divided into three distinct work habit types: dependent, independent, and interdependent (Covey 1990). It is helpful to know which type you are, so that you can be cognizant while communicating with other employees who are actually in the office and you are working in a virtual manner.

- Dependent employees rely on others to accomplish their goals. They often begin sentences with "you."
- Independent employees prefer to work alone and complete work goals without the help of others. They often begin sentences with "I."
- Interdependent employees enjoy working in teams to accomplish goals. They often begin their sentences with "we."

Is Working from Home a Good Fit for You?

Are you tired of commuting into the office every day and dealing with the same office politics? Have your increased spending costs for gas, lunch, and work clothes taken a bigger chunk out of your paycheck each pay period? Wouldn't it be great to grab a morning wake-up beverage of choice from your kitchen, walk into your home office, turn on your personal computer, and begin working? Well, maybe you can. To determine if working from home is a good fit for you, consider the following.

- How strong is your desire to work from home? The more you want to succeed at it, the more likely you will weather whatever difficulties arise.

- What importance do you place on your relationships with coworkers? If the social interaction at your office is one of your favorite things about your current job, you may feel isolated working at home. If, on the other hand, you're happiest when people leave you alone, you may thrive on the solitude of working at home. Moreover, maybe you can create a schedule for which you go into the office two or three days per week and you work from home for the balance.
- How well can you adapt to doing many different tasks each day? When you work at home, you will likely be responsible for everything from answering the phone to taking out the trash.
- Are you the sort of person who keeps everything in its place? Organized people will have an advantage when it comes to keeping up with reams of paperwork without secretarial or support staff.
- Do you love what you do? People who love what they do are less likely to procrastinate.
- What about the space where you live? Do you enjoy spending time there, and do you have adequate space in which to set up a home office?
- How do others in your household feel about you working at home? It helps if your family or housemates are supportive of your decision to work at home.

Key Tips for Working from Home

Set up a regular work schedule. Don't necessarily change your work mind-set; consider working at home just as you would work in an office. The work is still important, and part of a person's psychological well-being is being able to maintain a schedule. Creating and maintaining a schedule makes your designated time at work valuable to others. It will limit interruptions and time stealers.

Stay focused. Working at home is much more comfortable than working in an office, but the distractions are also much more tempting and prevalent. It is easy to be distracted by cleaning the house, watching television or slipping into an afternoon nap. This isn't a sign of laziness but one of losing sight of the tasks at hand and mixing up the priorities (Cottrell, Carnes, and Layton 2003).

Make social contact a part of your daily schedule. Many people who work from home feel disconnected from other people. This can lead to discouragement and depression. Avoid this by making a point to schedule business lunches, attend professional meetings, and maintain regular contact with customers or colleagues via telephone.

This may sound simple enough, but there is still a potential barrier to overcome: convincing your manager that working from home is in your best interest and that of the organization.

1

Convincing Your Manager

Your plans to convince your manager of your work-from-home ambitions should be deliberate and well planned. You may have only one opportunity to convince your manager, if your position is not already being structured to work off premises. This is no time for an "elevator speech" in passing.

Know Your Manager's Paradigm

Before you enter into a discussion about your plans, evaluate where your manager may be coming from. Many people do not understand the benefits that working at home can provide. Some people have an older stereotype of working, based on past experience (Covey 1990); they believe that work only gets done at the organization's facility. While this is true for some jobs, there are many jobs with tasks that can be done remotely.

- Marriott reservations are completed by 325 employees working from their homes (Kimo Kippen, personal communication 2010).
- Accounting firm KPMG (formerly, Klynveld, Peat, McClinton, and Goerdeler) creates all its training materials

through employees working from home with a secured, social Web site where they can see each other's work and where feedback from subject matter experts can be input and viewed (Daniel Kuzup, personal communication 2010).

- Hewlett-Packard technical support is provided by technical experts working from their homes around the world, even though you are calling a toll-free phone number in the United States (Robert Gordon, personal communication 2010).

Make a list of all the daily/weekly tasks required for your job. Evaluate which tasks can be completed remotely, and mark each with an *H*. Mark tasks that must be completed on the premises with *O*s.

Prepare your notes carefully so that you can articulate them clearly with your manager. Once your manager has made a decision regarding your request to work from home, be sure that you understand the reasoning behind his/her decision. This is significant, in case there is an opportunity to revisit the conversation. Be accepting of your manager's decision, and don't get defensive or confrontational. You never want to burn a bridge, regardless of the outcome of the decision.

Once you have specifically outlined your conversation, consider when and where it should take place; those are important factors as well.

Timing and Location

If your manager is putting out many fires, expecting important visitors, or scheduled in back-to-back meetings all day long, recognize that it would probably not be a good time to talk. This is not the type of conversation to conduct in the hallway or with other employees present. The best approach is to schedule a thirty-minute meeting in the manager's office. If your manager asks, "What is this about?", reply with a generic statement like, "I want to discuss some ideas about my job" as opposed to "I would like to talk about working from home".

Being a skilled communicator can make the difference between a yes and a no response.

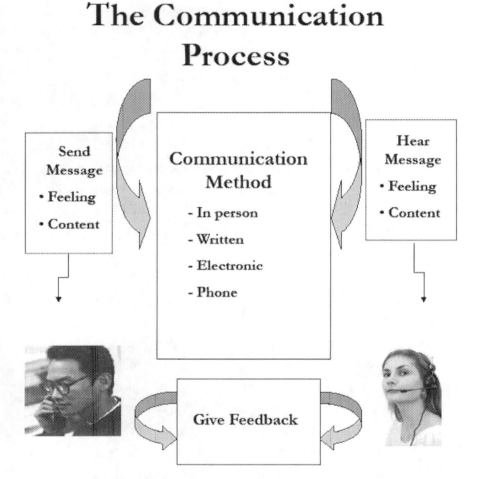

The Communication Process

Communication Skills

Effective communication is a complex process including several basic skills. Communication is not a science of regimented, precise procedures. There are specific, sound principles and themes, but there are thousands of variations on these themes, which can be construed subjectively by the intended receiver(s). The most critical type of communication is face-to-face. That's when you are persuading others by communicating your ideas in person (Decker 1996).

Your believability is critical to the successful outcome of a persuasive conversation. No matter what is said, it is not going to make much difference in the mind of the listener unless you are credible and believable. On that note, there are three distinct components of a message that can lead to your believability (Mehrabian 1993).

The three components of a message that need to be consistent to make the presenter believable are: verbal, vocal, and visual. The verbal component is the actual words used. The tone component represents the tone, pitch, and vocal quality of the message. The visual component refers to speaker's body language. Which component most influences the listener's judgment of your believability?

- Verbal: 7 percent
- Vocal: 38 percent
- Visual: 57 percent

The actual words (verbal component) lead to your believability in a small way.

However, your voice and body language contribute greatly to your believability. When all three elements work together, your message is consistent. The excitement and enthusiasm of your voice work with the energy and animation of your face and body to reflect your confidence and conviction. If you are nervous or under pressure, you will most likely concentrate on your words while your voice may come across as halting and tremulous. You are more likely to look down and clasp your hands. Be aware that these (sometimes natural) behaviors send an inconsistent message, eroding your believability.

Colin Powell was relatively unknown when the American people wanted him to run for president. What made him such an attractive candidate and liked by so many people? He made the verbal, vocal, and visual elements of his message work together, hence making him believable in the eyes of the American people.

Former presidents Bill Clinton and Ronald Reagan couldn't have been any more different from each other. From their political parties to their political views to their ages, they were on opposite ends of the spectrum. But they had one thing in common: they sent consistent messages through their words, voice, face, and body, making them believable to the American people.

Decker (1996) identified nine behavioral skills that, when displayed well, can help you send a consistent message. You use these skills every day, but you may not be aware of them.

Eye communication is the most important tool you have in your personal-impact toolkit. Effective eye communication includes standing or sitting no closer than three feet away from the person with whom

 you are conversing and maintaining three to five seconds of direct eye contact before you look away for a moment. If you are uncomfortable looking directly at people's eyes, try looking at their foreheads. This will have the same effect.

Practice Activities

1. Have a "stare-down" with a partner. Sit or stand three feet apart. Make eye contact with your partner while your partner silently counts the seconds you maintain eye contact without looking away. When you reach five seconds of constant eye contact, have your partner raise a hand to indicate the five-second mark. Keep trying until you have maintained five seconds of constant eye contact.

2. Add voice to the stare-down. Try the same exercise as above, but talk to your partner while maintaining five seconds of constant eye contact.

Posture sends a critical message as to whether you are really engaged and passionate about what you are saying or whether you really want to be there. Your posture, sitting or standing, is often attributed to the habits you had when you were a teenager (Dr. Jon Sherman, personal communication 2006). You may have slumped your shoulders because you were tall or shy and wanted to fit in with everyone. Maybe you slouched in a chair when sitting because you were nervous about speaking to someone one-on-one.

Effective posture when sitting includes aligning your back with the back of the chair, keeping your feet flat on the floor and your arms resting on chair arms or on your lap without crossing or clasping your hands together. When standing, use the ready position just as athletes do. In the ready position, your feet should be flat on the floor, shoulder-width apart; your knees should be slightly bent as if you could move at any moment in any direction, and your arms should be relaxed and at your sides. Avoid shifting your weight to one hip, crossing your feet, rocking from heel to toe, pacing, and clasping your hands in front of you, because those behaviors send a message of noninterest.

Practice Activities

1. Look at yourself sitting and standing in front of a mirror. This activity is even better if someone can videotape you. Practice effective and ineffective ways so you can see what message others see.
2. Walk away from a wall. Stand against a wall with your heels and shoulders touching the wall and hands at your side. Slowly relax and allow your lower back to touch the wall.

Maintaining this body position, take a few steps away from the wall. Shake your hands slightly so you will not be so stiff, and take a few more steps. Does this posture make you feel more confident? That's the message others will see.

Gestures and facial expressions reflect energy when you communicate. You should have your arms and hands natural and relaxed when you are at rest. You gesture naturally when you are animated and enthusiastic. Learn to smile under pressure in the same way you would with a natural smile when you are comfortable. Gestures need to be natural for you. Avoid low-energy gestures that may appear when you're nervous, such

as clasping your hands low and in front of your body, clasping your hands at waist level, and placing your hands on your hips. A smile may come naturally to you, or it may not. If you are not a natural smiler, you need to be aware of your most important facial gesture. Stand in front of a mirror and make a smile that looks natural for you. Then close your eyes to remember how it feels so you can repeat it in front of other people—not just the mirror.

Practice Activities

1. Talk in front of a mirror, sitting and standing, as if the mirror is another person. Look for your most natural gestures and facial expressions. Look for any bad habits that may erode your confidence and energy levels. Keep practicing until you see natural gestures and facial expressions without bad habits. Better yet, have someone videotape you.

2. Watch a situation comedy (sitcom), the news, or a talk show on television with the sound off for about ten minutes.

See if you can determine what the people on television are communicating without hearing their words. Their believability, confidence, and credibility are largely conveyed through their gestures and facial expressions.

Dress and appearance send a message within the first five seconds of meeting a person. They say, "Never judge a book by its cover," but people do. Those initial five seconds are known to provide an emotional impression rather than a content or intellectual impression. Since 90 percent of your body is covered by clothing, be aware of what your clothing and appearance are communicating. The 10 percent not covered also draws people to form impressions. Be aware of your grooming habits, hairstyle, jewelry, cosmetics, tattoos, and facial hair.

Dress appropriately, even though you may not have a guidebook that tells you how to groom and dress for certain types of occasions. You should choose comfortable clothing that is in sync with the company's culture but also consider the climate, time of day, social situation, and  other circumstances. Be sure your clothes fit well and are not outdated, and choose colors and patterns that accentuate your body type and skin tone. Dress and appearance may seem superficial, but they communicate to others how you feel about yourself.

Practice Activities

1. Go to a place where lots of people gather, such as a store, sporting event, public building, etc. Observe the dress and appearance of five people you do not know for five seconds and analyze what impressions you can draw from them in that five seconds.

2. Every day, look for something new in a new way. Choose an item such as your shoes, dress, suit, slacks, jacket, tie, shirt, and/or a grooming habit. Change it. Combine it with something different from what you have been combining it with. Dressing differently daily will sensitize you to how you feel about your dress and appearance.

Voice and vocal variety is the primary vehicle that carries your message. It's literally the vehicle surrounding your words—you can have an old jalopy that rattles down the road or a smoothly running, finely tuned automobile. Both will get you to your destination, but the quality of the ride varies greatly. Your voice transmits energy. The excitement and enthusiasm you feel should be directly conveyed by the sound of your voice. Record your voice to become aware of how much energy you

 transmit to others. The quality of your vocal tone and variety can count for 84 percent of your believability when people cannot see you, such as on a telephone call (Mehrabian 1992). Subtleties of voice are far more numerous than you may think. You can read an enormous amount into the vocal tone of people during the first few seconds on the phone.

There are four aspects that make up your vocal expression: relaxation, breathing, resonance, and projection. Each can be altered through exercises to expand your vocal expression. They all work together to give your voice its unique characteristics. Vocal variety is a great way to keep people interested and involved. Use the roller coaster to consciously raise your voice and let it plummet. This will make you aware of a monotone. Don't read speeches, as that often leads to a monotone delivery.

Practice Activities

1. Call five companies at random out of the phone book. Rate them on their vocal tone and the quality of the way they answer the phone.

2. Increase your resonance. Drop your jaw and allow it to hang loosely. Inhale deeply through your nose, allowing your belly to fill with air. As you exhale say, "King Kong. Ding dong. Bing bong." Begin with a high tone and gradually lower your tone for each word. Do this gently, and avoid pushing on your throat muscles.

3. Several relaxation activities that may improve your voice can be found in the chapter on maintaining balance.

Language, pauses, and nonwords are most associated with the verbal component of your believability, but they often become distractions for your listeners. Language is made up of both words and nonwords such as um, ah, and jargon that fill otherwise quiet space. You communicate most effectively when you are able to select the right words and use direct language to state your intentions. This requires you to have a rich vocabulary that can be used responsively and appropriately as the situation and audience demand. For example, you would not talk to a child the same way as you would a group of physicians.

Nonwords are barriers to clear communication. Um, okay, you know, well, and, etc., are not just sloppy but distracting when repeated as a habit. Replace these nonwords with pauses. Pauses are an integral part of language. Effective communicators use pauses between sentences.

Outstanding communicators use pauses for dramatic effect, even in the middle of a sentence.

Pauses allow you to emphasize key points of your conversation. They can also bring the wandering-minded listener back to listening to you. Effective pauses are usually three to four seconds long. However, pauses can be uncomfortable when you are sending your message. You may think these few seconds seem like a few hours. You may feel compelled to fill the silence with ums and ahs, but try to wait out the silence with a pause.

Beware of jargon. Jargon is excellent communication shorthand for people who share the same language. Even English words will sound like a foreign language if your listener doesn't understand your jargon. Learn to use and pronounce words correctly.

Speak the language of your manager. The words you choose and the tone with which you deliver the message should be crafted to inspire interest in your manager. Managers have key organizational performance measures that they monitor quite closely. But they tend to gravitate toward one more than the others. Performance measures may include:

- financial goals;
- employee development;
- workplace safety;
- diversity;
- customer feedback;
- employee engagement/satisfaction;
- human resources administration;
- labor hours;
- inventory management;
- receivables (money owed to the company by customers or clients);
- asset management (property held that depreciates over time and may be paid for against an amortization schedule); and
- growth.

Does your manager emphasize one of these performance indicators? If so, this would be an angle from which to craft your words and tone. Your manager is more likely to listen to you if you are speaking from a base that really matters to him/her.

Practice Activities

1. Use one new word in your conversations every day. Find a half-dozen times when you can use that word. Try words such as dissemble, jocular, fulsome, robust, espouse, etc. The words do not need to be long or intellectual, just different. Make your own list, and work on it daily.

2. With a partner, explore how pauses feel for you. Sitting or standing in front of your partner, say the sentences "My name is…" (pause) "I am from …" (pause) "I work at …" with a four-second pause between each one. While you are speaking, your partner should visually count on his/her fingers about how many seconds have elapsed. After four seconds, say the next sentence and pause again.

3. Have a colleague observe a conversation you may be having with a customer, coworker, vendor, manager, or on the phone. The colleague should provide you with feedback on the length of the conversation and how many nonwords you used.

Listener involvement, when executed well, can greatly enhance a listener's comprehension of your message. You could simply provide

content that reaches the linear processing (left) part of your listener's brains. But when you are involved in interpersonal communication, you are revealing ideas and opinions. You are trying to move a person to action or persuade him/her to agree. If you miss involving your listener's creative (right) part of the brain, you are missing part of your potential impact. Listeners—whether one person in a conversation or hundreds of people composing an audience—are bombarded with stimuli every instant. You need to engage all of their senses. The more involved a listener is, the more you can convince and persuade him/her.

A "swirl" is a moment of total involvement in the mind of the learner. A swirl can be a laugh, a mental aha, completing an exercise related to your message, having to think of a question, deciding whether or not to volunteer, and so forth. Many swirls can be created. Here a few examples:

- Create drama by using a strong opening, announcing a serious problem or startling fact, telling a moving story, or asking a rhetorical question to get your listeners thinking.
- Use your effective eye communication.
- Change the dynamic of your conversation with personal movement (a step forward, to the side, or to a visual aid)—but no bad habits.
- Add variety by using multiple types of visual aids.
- Use a variety of questions—ask rhetorical questions, ask for a show of hands in response to a question, ask for a volunteer to answer a question.
- Use a demonstration relevant to your message.
- Provide samples and gimmicks (food samples to taste, product samples) or create a metaphor in your message with jelly beans, M&M's, skittles, props, or costumes.
- If your listeners are beginning to fade out, engage their interest with drama, humor, or movement.
- Insert humor into your message. Try a friendly, warm comment about yourself. Don't tell jokes unless you know you are good at it. It is estimated that one in one hundred people are actually funny when telling jokes. Tell stories,

refer to current events, use one-liners, and poke fun at yourself. If you make a mistake, don't get nervous; laugh at yourself. With any of these techniques, keep it appropriate and professional.

Practice Activities

1. Watch some television talk show hosts and notice how they continuously involve their listeners and guests. They move around; ask questions; engage listeners through eye communication; and use gimmicks, props, visuals, and humor.

2. Take each of the listener-involvement techniques and apply one in your work life each day. When you complete the cycle, start again so that, each day, you're consciously aware of making an effort to involve people. Before long, listener involvement will become one of your positive habits.

Humor is an important attribute for interpersonal communication. Some people are naturally humorous, and others need to work at it, but humor is learnable.

You can be funny, humorous, and human when you open yourself up to be vulnerable, to be part of the human comedy. There is much to be gained in interpersonal communication by telling humorous asides, stories, anecdotes, and reactions.

In most interpersonal communications, comedy is not your end goal. Rather, your objective is to connect with your listeners on a personal level. That connection is made on a level of likeability and commonality. This can stem from being personal, open, friendly, caring, interested, personable, emotional, concerned, pleasant, comfortable, confident, unselfish, and fun. So add humanity to your humor.

When you are talking, people look at your face. Your most dominate facial feature is your smile. This important feature of your physiognomy quickly shows if you are excited, enthusiastic, angry, serious, or somewhere in between. Your sense of humor is perceived nonverbally through your smile. It is important to know your natural smile.

Some of the most effective swirls come during moments of lightness or involvement. Those emotional moments are the best times to get your message across. You reach both the left side and right side of the brain when you use humor and humanization.

Practice Activities

1. Find out more about your sense of humor. Do you have a dry wit, or do you like earthy stories? Do you have an infectious laugh or exhibit an easy smile? Everybody is different, yet most love to laugh and have fun. Find out what your humor profile is. Ask others to rate your sense of humor on a scale of one to ten.

2. Keep a humor journal. In your journal, keep a page for quotes, anecdotes, stories, and funny things that happen in your daily life. Consciously keep it for a week, writing down ten light items in your life each day. If you don't find ten, work harder at humor. Life is meant to be joyful.

Showing the natural self is not a single skill; rather, it is a way to use all the skills in a way that suits your personality. Think of the most forceful speaker you know. Think of the best leader you know. In each case, you will not find one who is a copy of anyone else. Everyone is different. Each person has his or her strengths and weaknesses. Although this seems like a simple concept, it gains complexity when you factor in the thousands of variables that impact interpersonal communications.

You have resources to draw on: your natural strengths that are already there and the areas to make into strengths.

If you ever learned to juggle, you probably began with one ball (just to get the rhythm) and then added another to practice working with both hands. Finally, you practiced adding a third ball until you could juggle. Becoming an expert in interpersonal communications is similar to juggling. You master one skill at a time and add more until they become a habit.

Acknowledge your natural strengths, and be thankful that you do not have to learn them from scratch. You may have an easy, natural smile, but others may need to work on lightening themselves up in their interpersonal communications. You may find it difficult to gesture naturally, while another might have been born talking with his/her hands. Recognize your strengths and work to improve and capitalize on them. Next work on your weaknesses, one at a time, until they become strengths. Take your weakest area first, and work to improve it every day for a week. For example, eye communication may be a difficult skill for you to master. Put your conscious mental energy into making extended eye communication each day for a week or two. Then move to another skill. Continue this process until you have improved all the skills.

No one is a perfect interpersonal communicator. You will find new, unwanted habits as well as old, undesirable habits that creep back. You will also find new strengths as you mature and as you experiment with various behavioral skills. Often, synergy occurs when a newfound habit works to improve an old habit. You may find that two habits work together to form an effective behavior. For example, movement and extended eye communication may breed confidence that allows you to maintain excellent eye communication with an individual and may even allow you to reach out and touch the shoulder of the listener.

Practice Activities

1. Show the list of skills to five individuals, and ask them to rank your demonstration of the skills from your greatest strength to your greatest weakness. Observe what others see in you. Compare responses with your self-perception. If they match, you know where to start work. If they do not match, take the areas that are least consistent and start with those.

2. Don't be satisfied. Keep working to improve your skills further.

Key Tips for Convincing Your Manager

Determine what you believe to be your manager's opinion about working from home. Analyze your current position to present solid evidence of tasks that you could complete from home. Share examples of companies with work from home employees. Schedule a meeting with your manager in his or her office to discuss your ideas.

Increase your believability through study and practice of the nine key communication skills Effective eye communication includes standing or sitting no closer than three feet away from the person with whom you are conversing and maintaining three to five seconds of direct eye contact before you look away for a moment. Posture sends a critical message as to whether you are really engaged and passionate about what you are saying or whether you really want to be there. You gesture naturally when you are animated and enthusiastic. Learn to smile under pressure in the same way you would with a natural smile when you are comfortable. Gestures need to be natural for you. Avoid low-energy gestures that may appear when you're nervous. Dress appropriately, even though you may not have a guidebook that tells you how to groom and dress for certain types of occasions.

Your voice transmits energy. The excitement and enthusiasm you feel should be directly conveyed by the sound of your voice. Language is made up of both words and nonwords that fill otherwise quiet space. You communicate most effectively when you are able to select the right words and use direct language to state your intentions. Replace these nonwords with pauses. Pauses allow you to emphasize key points of your conversation. The words you choose and the tone with which you deliver the message should be crafted to inspire interest in your manager. Involve your listener to move a person to action or persuade him/her to agree.

You can be funny, humorous, and human when you open yourself up to be vulnerable, to be part of the human comedy. There is much to be gained in interpersonal communication by telling humorous asides, stories, anecdotes, and reactions. Becoming an expert in interpersonal communications is similar to juggling. You master one skill at a time and add more until they become a habit. Acknowledge your natural strengths, and be thankful that you do not have to learn them from scratch.

2

Successfully Working from Home

Once you have convinced your manager that a work-from-home schedule will benefit you and the company, it's time to plan your success with an alternative work location. It's not as easy as you may think. You must be determined and disciplined in a few areas to be successful at working from home. People who telecommute from home often brag that they can wear their pajamas all day or never change out of their gym clothes. Be leery of such statements. Oftentimes, wearing pure leisure clothes can interfere with productivity for many people who work from home.

Setting Up Shop

Have an office room that is completely separate from any other home activities. It needs to be a space solely devoted to your work (i.e., no kids' toys, no household bills, no school or craft projects). Working in the kid's play area, in a workout area, or on the kitchen table or living room sofa may not lead to a productive day.

If you do not have an office set up in your home, plan to convert a single room to be a dedicated home office. Take a look at these tips if you're designing from scratch (eHow 2008. Make money from home, retrieved on line February 22, 2010 from _make-money-stay-home.html):

- Draw the outlines of the office or office space to scale on graph paper. A scale of one-quarter inch equals one foot usually works well.
- Mark anything that would affect your arrangement:
  - o electrical outlets
  - o phone jacks
  - o light switches
  - o windows
  - o doors that open into the room
- Make same-scale paper cutouts of your furniture, and shift them as needed until a likely arrangement emerges.
- Think about how you like to work. Some people must face the door or have a window view; others prefer to have fewer distractions.
- Be sure you have ample light, regardless of where you put your desk.
- Analyze what you do most frequently, and situate the furnishings accordingly. If you often search through file cabinets or reference books, keep them accessible.
- Place an ample surface near the telephone for note-taking.

There are many things you may take for granted while working on your company's premises. They are simply made available to you, probably by someone else. Plan on a trip to your local office supply store to purchase the standard office supplies you will need. Your current employer should not be expected to pay for these items when you work from home. Part of your convincing conversation with your manager was the financial benefits for the company, no matter how small.

Here are some office supplies you'll need:

Must Have

- a desk
- a chair
- shelves
- a file organizer
- pencils and pens
- a stapler and staples
- post-it notes or flags
- file folders
- a telephone
- a phone line dedicated to business, separate from your personal phone line
- a computer, unless your employer prefers you to use a company laptop (with a CD writer, most new PCs have them, but it is a necessity when working from home these days since some files are too large to e-mail and not every organization has an FTP site with which to transfer files)
- envelopes and delivery slips for overnight packages
- a printer with fax and scanner capability
- printer paper
- printer cartridges

Nice to Have

- a file cabinet
- measuring tape
- graph paper
- scissors
- a ruler
- a telephone headset
- an external hard drive for your computer; regular backups can be automatically performed (every evening)

- an account/relationship with a commercial courier service (UPS, FedEx, etc.)
- an uninterrupted power supply in the event that you lose power for a period of time; it allows you to run a PC, printer, or fax machine for about an eight-hour period

Besides separating your home office from other areas of your home, make the space cater to your need to focus on your work. Remove all distractions, such as home phone lines, televisions, pets, and clutter.

Make your work space comfortable. Invest in an ergonomic chair for sitting at your desk and for using your computer. You want your home office space to work for you; if you're comfortable in the office, you'll be less likely to escape to other areas of the house, where distractions can deter you from working.

Buy everything you can possibly afford to make your home office function as professionally as possible. This includes having a top-rated internet and e-mail service, a telephone with a headset, caller ID, and a phone company that has excellent messaging services that can be retrieved from another phone or a Blackberry.

Separate your home phone number from your business phone number. Do not answer your personal calls during your business hours.

Maintain a clutter-free desk. Think of your desk as a place of action, removing work at the end of each day and starting the next one fresh. Keep the minimum number of office supplies on your desk, and when possible, work on one project at a time to remain focused.

Make the best use of storage, which is often limited in a home office. If storage is at a premium, think about what you seldom use and move it to another storage area, such as the garage, attic, or basement. Consider installing a high shelf in the room—perhaps above the window or the closet door—for occasional-use reference books and supplies (extra file folders, computer paper, etc.).

Maintain the same child or elderly care arrangements you had when you were going to a company office site every day. Do not assume you can save money in care fees because you'll be at home. The cost to your productivity will be far greater.

Some Changes May Be Needed

When you begin working from home, you will likely jump at the chance to set your own hours and work in your pajamas if you feel like it. But you probably will not rush to sign up for the loneliness that a person working from home can experience. Feelings of isolation can keep you from focusing on work and can also be detrimental to your health (Vedantam 2006). There are a few things you can do to combat these feelings.

A good first step is to find a virtual support group. Seek out like-minded people online for support and guidance. You will find a wealth of Web sites and message boards dedicated to your specific business.

Maximize today's technology. Join a forum or a job networking site, or find some other way to connect with people in common situations online. These sites can provide information, support, and the interaction you need to stay connected to others. Monster.com is a generic job networking site, but most professional organizations have networking sites, or you can search Google for your specific business.

Join a professional organization. If your city or state has a business organization that matches your interest, join it. You'll make new contacts, be exposed to new ideas, and also make new friends. Go to meetings if the group meets together. It's an ideal way to overcome the isolation of working from home while also building your network.

Connect with colleagues and business friends. Pick up the telephone on a regular basis, and stay in touch with business friends and colleagues. E-mail is another good way to keep your friendships and connections. Most important of all, take an occasional lunch hour to meet with and socialize with your business friends. Face-to-face interaction will help you feel connected to others and offset feelings of separation.

Create a local support group if none exists. A work-at-home support group does wonders for the morale of the person who works at home. A group like that can offer support, advice and provide interaction and friendship—some common things that can be missing when working from home. Contact other friends who work at home and suggest getting together periodically.

From time to time, escape to an alternative work site. Instead of spending the work day at home alone, take your laptop, and work remotely from a different location that is conducive to working from a laptop. Local libraries, coffee shops, and universities usually have free wireless internet access available. Trying a different work site does three things:

- It gets you out of the house (and you know you need it!).
- It gets you in contact with other people.
- Changing the workspace helps alleviate boredom.

Get out of the house every day. Even if you're just walking around the block or checking the mail, leaving the house at least once daily can really help with isolation. Take a walk, run some errands, or take a drive around the neighborhood. The sunlight and change in scenery helps alleviate feelings of isolation (Editors of Consumer Reports Books 2008).

Same Old Routine

Treat working at home just as you would working in an office. In general, keep the same daily routines you had when you were going to the office. Go to bed at the same time, and wake up at the same time. There is a temptation to stay up later and sleep in longer when you are not expected at the office. Eat your meals and exercise on the same schedule.

Make sure you've shaved and showered before starting your day. Women who usually wear makeup when outside the home should put on a light, comfortable amount for working at home. Think of it as grooming for your job rather than grooming for those surrounding you in the office.

Get dressed for work. You'll find you'll get more done and feel more professional than if you're working in your office in your cozy pajamas. Save the sweats for the gym and the pajamas for the bed. While you want to feel comfortable, you don't want to be tempted to curl up and take a nap. A laid-back outfit can result in a laid-back attitude. Your coworkers might not see you while you're working from home, but continue your same routines for your job and your mental attitude.

Wear shoes. No one will know if you're barefoot, but having shoes on your feet has an important psychological impact on your work attitude. You'll feel as if you're out and about rather than relaxing at home.

Talk to your family and help them understand that, even though you appear to be home, you are not home. You work from home. Set aside an hour each day to focus on your family, perhaps when your children get home from school or your other family members arrive home after their day's activities. After that hour is up, go back to your home office and, if necessary, close the door.

Be prepared to respond appropriately to neighbors, friends, and acquaintances. Many people who have never worked from home before may not understand that you are doing serious work and that it is a real job. Take time to explain what you do when working from home, including the flexibility of your schedule, which allows you to take a walk or run errands in the middle of the day sometimes. Use your good interpersonal skills to help them understand the great discipline and commitment it takes to conduct business from home. You have to be firm, confident, and consistent when explaining the seriousness of what you do at home all the time.

Allow only package deliveries, business telephone calls, e-mails, doctor appointments, and emergencies to take you from your work. Laundry, house cleaning, electrical repairs, and gardening must be left until the evening or the weekend. During your work week, you work at home.

Prevent yourself from getting distracted. Even the most seasoned home-office professional feels the pull of the outdoors or wishes to leave work to do something fun. If you find yourself unable to concentrate, change into a business suit and sit back down at your desk. This will remind you that, if you were working at the office, you wouldn't have the option to take off to the spa or the golf course.

Once you have convinced your manager, set up your office, and are ready to implement some successful tips, focus your attention on productivity.

Key Tips for Successfully Working from Home

Dedicate one room in your home for an office, separate from all other home activities. If one does not exist, design one using the suggestions in this chapter. Purchase all the office supplies you anticipate needing. Make sure your work space is comfortable. Separate your home phone number from your business phone number. Maintain a clutter-free desk. Make the best use of storage. Maintain the same child or elderly care arrangements you had when you were going to an office site everyday.

You may need to change a few things to make working from home the most successful. Join a forum, job networking site, or other activities to connect with like-minded people on line as a support. Stay connected with colleagues and business friends by phone or face-to-face interactions. Learn from others who work from home. Try an alternate work site from home occasionally. Get out of the house at least once daily.

Treat working from home just as you would working at an office site. Keep the same schedules for sleeping, eating, and exercising. Practice the same routines for bathing, grooming, and dressing. Wear shoes. Talk to your family, housemates, and neighbors about your working schedule. Prevent yourself from getting distracted.

3

Improving Productivity

I mproving your productivity requires sharp focus. Focus is defined as directing energy toward a particular point or purpose. There are many external factors when working from home that can make it difficult for you to stay focused. In addition, business is a very complex and multifaceted arena, and the more complicated that becomes, the more difficult it is to remain focused. When you fail to maintain your focus, confusion and complexity increase. Don't spin your wheels trying to figure it out. Instead, take a moment to ask questions of others and yourself to restore your focus. Remember your primary focus is the issue at hand. Make sure that you can identify the main objectives of your job. When you can easily list those, you will find yourself better equipped to wade through the more challenging side of working from home, which is maintaining focus, despite the challenges and obstacles that will present themselves along the way.

Get More Done Each Day

Set office hours that provide you with structure when you are working from home. Keep a log of the work completed each day, along with a weekly account of time spent on specific projects or tasks. Send periodic status reports to your manager and any project team members, so they are aware of your accomplishments and the amount of time required for projects on which you worked. This gives you the flexibility of working from home while still having business objectives in focus.

Plan each work day in advance of beginning to work. For example, determine your daily objectives, and prioritize them for that particular day. You'll get more accomplished while working from home if you have a set agenda. You'll get off to a quick start rather than wasting time determining what to do next.

Develop a filing system. Create a file folder for each project, and file in a way that works for you, whether it's alphabetical or chronological. Place all file folders in a cabinet or organized container.

Take breaks. Every couple of hours, get a cup of tea, coffee, or water; make a phone call; or do a small task around the home. Breaks from the home office are important, because you don't have the natural interactions or distractions from other employees like you do when you are in a company office.

Think twice before trying to work out of your home with small children present. It can make a home office situation quite difficult. Not only will you find yourself wanting to spend time with the children— and away from work—you'll have to tend to their needs, keep them occupied, and face interruptions when trying to conduct business over the phone or through a meeting. Oftentimes, licensed, in-home day care providers can be found right in your neighborhood. This type of child care usually offers parents working from home more flexibility than traditional day care centers.

Manage both your work and your time well. One benefit to working from home is flexibility. However, that flexibility can easily get out of hand. Set daily business hours for yourself. Establish blocks of time when you will focus on your work and only your work. This schedule can be whenever you'd like it (depending on your job) from early morning to late at night. If you work during daylight hours, get up early in the morning and go straight to work on your most important task. You can often get more done before 8:00 AM than most people do in a day.

Keep track of deadlines and follow a work schedule to run a proper home office. You still have to satisfy your manager and colleagues. Decide how much work you have to do each day and then do it—no matter how long it takes.

Complete the most difficult tasks first. To defeat procrastination, learn to tackle your most unpleasant task(s) first thing in your work day instead of delaying it until later. This small victory will set the tone for a very productive day.

Determine your peak energy times. Once you have identified your highest cycles of productivity, schedule your most important tasks for those times. Work on minor tasks during your nonpeak times.

The most efficient way to get through a task is to delete it. If it doesn't need to be done, take it off your goal and priority list for the day.

Allocate uninterruptible blocks of time for solo work on which you must concentrate. Schedule light, interruptible tasks for your open-communication periods (e.g., when you know you are likely to receive the most phone calls during the day or week), and block out time for more challenging projects for your no-communication periods. Be sure to communicate these times to your manager and colleagues and document those blocked-off times in your electronic calendar so that others will know you are working but unavailable at that time. These time blocks may change depending on your priorities for any given day. However, be flexible--an often underrated, positive characteristic.

Create mini milestones. When you begin a task, identify the target you must reach before you can stop working. For example, when working on a report, white paper, or marketing brochure, you could decide not to get up until you've written at least one thousand words. Hit your target no matter what.

You could also use time-boxing: give yourself a fixed time period, such as thirty minutes, to make a dent in a task. Don't worry about how far you get. Just put in the time.

Batch similar tasks like making phone calls, printing, faxing, proofreading, copying, filing, or running errands into a time block, and complete them in a single session.

Create a cone of silence once in a while. Take a laptop with no network or Wi-Fi access, and go to a place where you can work without distractions, such as a library, park, coffee house, or your own backyard. Leave your communication gadgets behind.

Deliberately pick up the pace, and try to move a little faster than usual. Speak faster, walk faster, type faster, read faster, and then stop working sooner. Sometimes tasks aren't as scary or time-consuming as you initially make them out to be. Keep perspective. The Pareto Principle is the eighty-twenty rule, which states that 80 percent of the value of a task comes from 20 percent of the effort. Focus your energy on that critical 20 percent and don't overengineer the noncritical 80 percent. This is particularly important when you facilitate a meeting. Reduce procrastination and make decisions.

When you lead or facilitate a meeting (or conference call), be sure to provide clear, written agendas to meeting participants in advance. This greatly improves meeting focus and efficiency.

Reduce procrastination by taking action immediately after setting a goal, even if the action isn't perfectly planned. You can always adjust course along the way.

Once you have the information you need to make a decision, start a timer and give yourself just sixty seconds to make the actual decision. After sixty seconds, make a clear choice. Once your decision is made, take action to set it in motion. If you are still struggling with the final decision, go with your instinct. It's probably right.

Set a deadline for task completion, and use it as a focal point to stay on track. Tell others of your commitments, and they'll help hold you accountable.

Whatever it takes, start work when you when you told your manager you would when you were convincing him or her that you could work from home. If attending a live meeting, conference call, or video conference, be punctual, even arrive early.

Never have idle time. Catch up on reading when you are waiting for an appointment, standing in line, waiting for a conference call to begin, or even while your coffee or tea is brewing.

Visualize an objective as already accomplished. Put yourself into a state of actually being there. Make it real in your mind, and you'll soon see it in your reality.

Then give yourself frequent rewards for achievement. See a movie, book a professional massage, or spend a day at an amusement park—whatever it is that makes you feel good.

Separate the truly important tasks from the unimportant urgent ones. Allocate blocks of time to work on the critical tasks, those that are important but rarely urgent. Once you have delineated between important tasks and urgent ones, always squeeze in time for matters that are personally important to you, such as physical exercise, reading a book, or spending quality time, even by phone, with a loved one.

At the end of your workday, identify the first task you'll work on the next day, and set out the materials in advance. The next day, begin working on that task immediately.

Break complex projects into smaller, well-defined tasks. Focus on completing just one of those tasks at a time. Once you begin one of these smaller tasks, complete it 100 percent. Don't switch tasks in the middle, if possible. When distractions come up, jot them down to be dealt with later.

Pick a random piece of a larger project and complete it. Pay one random bill, make one phone call, or find an internet page where you can later review potential graphics for your project.

Identify a new habit you'd like to form, and commit to using that behavior for at least thirty days. A temporary commitment is much easier to keep than a permanent one.

Swap tasks with a colleague. Someone on your project team may have certain talents that allow him or her to complete a given task more quickly than you can. You may have talents that would allow you to complete that team member's task more efficiently. Be sure to communicate exactly what you want (format, layout, resources to use, etc.) and the precise time (date and time of day) when you need it completed.

Getting more done each day includes expanding your network outside of your industry by signing up for a martial arts course, starting a blog, joining an improvisational comedy group or a book club, taking tennis or golf lessons, or becoming a member at a gym. You'll often encounter ideas in one field that can boost your performance in another.

Identify the processes you use most often and write them down step-by-step. Refine them on paper to provide greater efficiency. Then, implement and test your improved processes. Sometimes you can't see what's right in front of you until you examine it under a microscope.

Avoid the urgency addiction. Urgent tasks are not always the most important. Do you pick up the phone every time it rings only to find the person on the other end of the line is a vendor wanting to sell you a new product that you don't necessarily need? Do you look at every e-mail as soon as it comes in, because you are notified by the beep from your computer? Do you make copies of a report as soon as you complete it and then return to the next one you need to do only to go to the copy machine again? Do you answer the door every time the doorbell rings only to find a package on your doorstep? These urgencies are often triggered by their sounds or a need to complete some of the repetitive tasks that will be completed on other projects the same day. Sort the less important tasks that may seem urgent at the time from the responsibilities that are truly most important.

Managing how much you get done each day can include a history of techniques. Covey, Merrill, and Merrill (1994) concluded that there are three generations of time management. The first generation is based on reminders. It's "go with the flow," but keep track of how you spend your time. This generation is characterized by simple notes and checklists. If you're in this generation, you carry these checklists with you and refer to them so you won't forget to do things. Hopefully, at the end of the day, you've accomplished many of the things you set out to do and you can cross them off your list. If some of these tasks are not completed, you put them on your list for tomorrow.

The second generation is one of planning and preparation. It's characterized by calendars and appointment books. It provides efficiency, personal responsibility, and achievement in goal-setting, planning ahead (tasks), and scheduling future activities and events (appointments). If you're in this generation, you make appointments, write down commitments, identify deadlines, and note where meetings will be held. You may do this on paper or on a computer.

The third generation approach is planning, prioritizing, and controlling. If you're in this generation, you've probably spent time clarifying your values and priorities. You've asked yourself, "What do I want?" You've set short-, medium-, and long-range goals aligned with your values. You prioritize your activities on a daily basis. This generation is characterized by a variety of planners and organizers—electronic as well as paper-based—with detailed forms for daily planning.

In many ways, these generations of time management have brought individuals a long way toward effectiveness in life. Such things as planning, prioritizing, clarifying values, and setting goals have made a significant positive difference.

J. Meredith (2007 The fourth generation of time management. Champions Club Community, retrieved on line March 24, 2010 from www.covey.championsclubcommunity.com/2009/07/12/four-generations-of-time-management/) has revealed a fourth generation of time management. He concludes that this generation of time management is not to manage time but to manage oneself. Expectation (and satisfaction) lies in an individual's scope of influence. Fourth-generation expectations focus on preserving and enhancing relationships, accomplishing results, and maintaining balance.

The goal of time management is not to schedule work but to use time effectively to achieve goals so that human relations and enjoyment of spontaneity are not lost to mechanical obsession with so-called efficiency.

Use Multiple Methods to Communicate

You have numerous methods with which to communicate. Using them appropriately can increase your productivity. In an environment where time is critical and employees need to be productive whether they are in the office, a hotel room, an airport, the home, or another city, state, or country, technology has come to the rescue—but not without a steep learning curve. E-mail, voice mail, conference calls, and video conferencing have revolutionized the communication processes in corporate America and around the world. Dependency on these technologies has become increasingly more important as more and more employees work on virtual teams. Yet, training on how and when to use these technologies has been limited.

E-mail

E-mail is the preferred method of written communication, with the number of e-mails surpassing the number of letters sent through the United States Postal Service (*US News and World Report* 2008). Since individuals who receive your e-mails do not have the benefit of hearing the tone in your voice, observing your body language, or seeing your facial expressions and may not be familiar with your communication style, what they read is what they get—in black and white.

Organizational structures have become very complex and matrix-like. You may send an e-mail to an individual or group with whom you have not yet built a relationship and consequently, you are not familiar with one another's communication styles and/or you may be unsure about where this individual or group fits within the organization. In this situation, you should carefully consider the various communication styles and diverse backgrounds that make up organizations.

Because e-mail is easily accessible and is easy to use, it is a fast way to send and receive information and has somewhat of an informal feel to it. Executives rarely spend as much time formulating messages or responses to messages by e-mail as they would with a message that is perceived as more formal (Benson 2009). It is critical that you keep your e-mail messages clear, concise, and focused on facts. Before you begin crafting a message, review the following:

- Consider the objective of your message. Make sure e-mail is the appropriate vehicle to send your message. A conference call or video conference may be more appropriate or achieve better results.
- The overall guiding principle is to think before sending your message. Be sure you know what you want to say and what you want to achieve by sending the message.
- If the recipients of your message don't know who you are, introduce yourself in the beginning of the message (name, address, phone number and e-mail address) or contact them first by phone or voicemail to introduce yourself and explain what you need. A few other significant protocols are necessary:
- Never send bad news or a harsh message through e-mail.
- Don't say anything that you would not say to the individual in person.
- Don't debate a topic through e-mail. Place a phone call where all parties can share their perspectives and resolve any conflicts. This will yield the desired outcome more quickly.

- If you receive negative feedback or sense frustration from an e-mail you've received, do not respond immediately. When you are ready to discuss the issue or issues at hand, do so by telephone.
- Be certain that the individuals you select to put in the "To" box need to read and/or act on your message. Individuals listed in the "cc" box are receiving the message as an FYI. In the "subject" box, indicate if the message is "ACTION REQUIRED" or "NO ACTION REQUIRED." Begin the body of the message by clearly stating why the recipients are getting the communication, what action they need to take, and how much time you expect that action to take (your deadline).
- Messages should focus on facts, not opinions and emotions.
- If you are sending a lengthy message, create it like an outline with more detail in collapsible sections or attached documents (Benson 2009).
- Always proofread your message to correct misspellings and grammatical errors. Careless errors imply that the sender does not care.
- Check any text that you are copying into your message to ensure that everything was copied, including punctuation.
- Different colors, fonts, and graphics can dramatically increase the size of the file. Large files take longer to retrieve and open. If possible, post large files to a Web site and include a link to it (Benson 2009).
- Avoid using aggressive punctuation such as the exclamation mark or all capital letters, as that can be interpreted as yelling. Refrain from using slang, abbreviations, acronyms, and offensive language. Do not send chain letters, and generally speaking, share jokes with family and friends rather than professional colleagues.

- If someone sends you three messages, each on a different subject, consider replying with just one e-mail addressing all three topics.
- Not only do you need to work on effective message writing, you need to manage all the e-mails others send you. Don't be a slave to the new-message sounds and visuals. Turn the sound off on your computer. Schedule set times throughout the day when you will review and respond to new e-mails. Initially, this might be a difficult habit to form, but it is a very efficient time-management strategy.

When checking your e-mail, categorize your e-mail messages immediately. Delete junk mail first. As soon as you reply to a message, delete it if you will not need to reference it again. Delete messages that you no longer need. Mailbox maintenance can be quite consuming if you do not keep up with it.

Voice Mail

Voice mail allows you to send and receive messages remotely from any phone in the world. Through a combination of e-mail and voice mail, an executive could go several days without talking voice-to-voice with anyone and yet get the job done—and get it done quickly regardless of what time it is. Voice mail is a more personal, informal communication, because the receiver hears your voice and vocal tones.

Determine if voice mail is the most appropriate vehicle for your message. Because voice mail offers only one-way communication, you need to be careful that your message won't leave too many unanswered questions.

Speak clearly and confidently. Put your best voice forward but be natural, just as you would when speaking with someone in person. Add some of your personality as appropriate through voice inflections and laughter. While the recipients can hear your voice, they still cannot see your body language. Keep your message as brief as possible. Begin your voice mail with your name, organizational role, contact number, and the objective of the message, especially if action is required on the part of the recipient. Close your message by restating your name, organizational role, and contact number. Do not speak too quickly, especially when leaving your phone number. Listen to your recorded message to make sure you are satisfied with it before sending the message. If you are forwarding a message from another person, provide a brief explanation in an introductory message. If you need an immediate response to your message, mark it as urgent, but don't abuse the privilege.

If you are sending a lengthy voice mail message:

- Make an outline for yourself to help guide you when you are recording the message. Keep this outline in case you need to answer questions later for the recipient.
- Manage expectations about the length of the message by stating in the beginning that it is a lengthy message, how many key points will be addressed, how many minutes it will take to listen to it, and that the recipient can save the message to listen to later because it is important to hear the entire message.

If you send messages frequently to the same group of people, establish a distribution list. You may want to send a message to yourself first to edit and then forward to your group. In the event you press a wrong button and lose the message, you would not have to record the message again.

While mobile phones are popular for conducting business, they can present some challenges when sending voice mail. If you have a short message to send, the background noise on a mobile phone is probably acceptable. Do not attempt to send a long, detailed message on a mobile phone, because you could lose connection, and background noise can be a distraction (Mayer 2002). Your recipient may have to listen to your message several times or call you for clarification, causing frustration for them and wasted time for you.

Your phone needs some additional management. If you will be away from your phone for an extended period of time, change your recorded message to inform callers of when you will return and who they can contact in your absence. If you will be unable to send a message at a particular time, record a message in advance and queue it to be delivered at a certain date and time. Try to return voice mail messages within twenty-four hours. If you need to research an answer to a caller's request, call them and let them know that you received the message and inform the caller of when he/she can expect an answer back from you.

Do not use voice mail:

- to deliver bad news or a harsh message;
- to avoid talking with someone;
- to avoid or resolve conflict; or
- that contains offensive language.

Conference Calls

Conference calls are similar to meetings, only virtual. Conference calls allow virtual teams to maintain communication and stay productive. These virtual meetings are less expensive than face-to-face meetings and provide an opportunity for team members to offer and receive more information, more informally than e-mail. More and more companies are opting to use conference calls over face-to-face meetings, because they can be more efficient and less costly. A business professional spends an average of three hours per day in meetings. Face-to-face meetings can cost up to seven times more than meetings conducted through conferencing technology (Benson 2009). Additionally, the use of conference calls has risen from 27 percent in 2000 to 48 percent in 2009 (*Chicago Tribune* 2009). At some point, if not already, you may be a participant in a conference call or even the leader of one.

<u>Leading the Conference Call</u>

Like a face-to-face meeting, effective conference calls require strong facilitation skills in the leader, including general knowledge about the participants on the call and the subject of the call, and active participation from and good listening skills in all involved. Conference calls can be by phone only, by a webcast that requires all participants to use computers so the leader can share his/her screen with them while walking them through a presentation that may include graphics, charts, and participant polling (a show of virtual hands in response to a question)—or all three. You should prepare for a conference call much the same way you would for a face-to-face meeting with a few additions:

- Clearly document the objective and desired outcomes of the conference call, and make sure a conference call is the best forum to carry your message.

- Set the date and length of time for the conference call; ninety minutes is the maximum length before participants begin to lose focus and need a break. Schedule the conference call or webcast with your conferencing vendor and obtain a dial-in number and/or a webcast link.

- Create an agenda that includes the what, who, and time allotted for each topic along with desired outcomes/action. Send an e-mail invitation that contains the start and end time of the call and the required dial-in number or code to the conference call attendees at least two weeks in advance. Include as a separate attachment the agenda and any prereading materials. Ask participants to plan on dialing or signing in five to ten minutes in advance of the call start time in case there are any technical difficulties, particularly for webcasts, so you can begin the conference call on time.

Effective conference calls involve only people who can make significant contributions to the process. Marginal contributors, spectators, curiosity seekers, lost souls, and troublemakers should be left out.

- Using a telephone with a headset is very helpful; speakerphones have their setbacks, and with a headset you are hands-free for when you have to write a note, access your computer to reference something, etc.
- Conduct a preparation conference call with the speakers/ presenters to ensure everyone is clear on the outcomes/ expectations and their roles during the conference call.
- Begin the conference call on time, engage all participants throughout the call, allow five minutes to summarize the call (even if you have not covered all topics from the agenda), and end the conference on time.
- Have an employee, who is not involved in the discussion, take notes during the conference call, or prearrange for your conference call– or webcast-provider to record and transcribe the call.
- If you run out of time before discussing all agenda issues, place those items on the agenda for the next conference call.
- Send minutes from the conference call to participants within forty-eight hours after the call. The participants who attended the conference call or webcast do not need to read a complete narrative of the event, but they do need to review decisions made and further action that is necessary. A quick way to create minutes is to add three additional columns to your agenda labeled "decision/further action," "who," and "when."

Table 3.1 Sample Agenda

What	Who	Time	Desired Outcome	Further Action Required (Minutes)		
				What	Who	When
Introductions	All	10 minutes	Get to know the team			
Financial update	Maria	15 minutes	Understand the full-picture baseline			
New product demo	Tom	20 minutes	Determine market potential			
Marketing strategy	All, Juan facilitates	25 minutes	Brainstorm marketing ideas			
Process improvement project	Dan	15 minutes	Lessons learned to be applied to future projects			
Revised HR policies	Myah	15 minutes	Updates to policy manual			
Birthday and service awards	Kimo	15 minutes	Celebrate			
Summary	Carla	5 minutes	Summarize decisions made and further action to be taken			

Participating in a Conference Call

Participating in a conference call requires some etiquette to respect all participants and to help keep the virtual meeting focused.

- Review all materials sent for the conference call or webcast in advance and write down questions and discussion points you have.

- Give the call your undivided attention. Avoid the temptation to multitask, because that may create more work later by missing some important discussions.
- Unless absolutely necessary, do not dial in from a mobile phone. Mobile phones can have poor reception and distract other participants with an excess of background noise. If you must use a mobile phone, let the facilitator know.
- If you are using a speakerphone, place it on mute when others are speaking to limit background noise.
- State your name before interjecting yourself into the discussion.
- If your phone plays music when a caller is placed on hold, do not place the phone on hold during the conference call.

Video Conferencing

Video conferences, though more expensive than conference calls, offer some clear advantages, including enhanced communication, the ability to see all participants receiving your message, and the ability to conduct a virtual face-to-face meeting with either limited or no travel expenses (Mayer 2002). This technology offers a more personal way of delivering your message. Video conferencing is best used when you need to reach thousands of people in two cities or in multiple countries. Some of the best applications include a CEO who wants to reach all employees, personally, with an important message as well as training seminars at companies, colleges, and universities.

Just as in a face-to-face meeting, a video conference enables facilitators, speakers, and all participants to use white boards, presentation slides, and body language to help get their messages across. A good video conference feels just like a good face-to-face meeting. A video conference is a bit more challenging to lead than a conference call due to the equipment and space needs. But don't let that stop you. An adequate meeting room with the necessary equipment and internet accessibility is all you need. Preparing and conducting a video conference is much the same as you preparing and conducting a face-to-face meeting, with a few additional steps.

- Clearly document the objective and desired outcomes for the video conference, and make sure a video conference is the best forum to carry out your message.

- Set the date and length of time for the video conference; four hours with scheduled breaks is the maximum length before participants begin to lose focus. Schedule the video conference with your video conferencing vendor. Work through the technical aspects and logistics for the video conference, and reserve an appropriate space.

- Create an agenda that includes the what, who, time allotted for each topic, and desired outcomes/action. Send an e-mail invitation to the video conference at least three weeks in advance with the agenda and prereading materials as attachments to your message. Ask participants to submit their questions three days in advance of the video conference and to plan on connecting ten to fifteen minutes in advance of the conference start time, in case there are any technical difficulties, so you can begin the conference on time.

- Identify an individual in each location who can host the video conference onsite. This person can reserve an appropriate space, help with communication, arrange for necessary equipment (based on the recommendations from your video conferencing supplier), ensure handouts are ready, etc. More importantly, this person can be onsite, making sure that things run smoothly and resolving any issues that may arise.

- Send a reminder e-mail with the agenda and prereading attachments one week in advance.

- Conduct a preparation conference call with the speakers/ presenters to ensure that everyone is clear on the outcomes/ expectations and their roles during the video conference.
- Conduct a timed trial run of the video conference presentation.
- Plan to arrive at the video conference space thirty minutes prior to the onset of the conference to test the equipment and ensure that everything is working and that the materials are in place.
- Begin the video conference on time, engage all locations throughout the conference, allow for the last five minutes of the conference to be a summary of the meeting (even if you have not covered all topics from the agenda), and end the conference on time.
- Have an employee, who is not involved in the discussion, take notes during the video conference or prearrange for additional broadcasts of the video conference through your video conference provider.
- If you run out of time to finish before discussing all issues, place the missed items on the agenda for another video conference call.
- Send minutes of the conference call to participants within forty-eight hours after the call. The participants who attended the conference call or webcast do not need to read a complete narrative of the event, but they do need to review decisions made and further action that is necessary. A quick way to create minutes is to add three additional columns to your agenda labeled "decision/further action," "who," and "when."

As a presenter at a video conference, you should present as if at a face-to-face meeting. Do not wear distracting colors or patterns. Certain colors, especially white, and patterns (stripes, plaids, small and busy) tend to react adversely to light and may distort the image that is seen by your participants. Do not let the camera intimidate or distract you.

A video conference participant needs to follow a few etiquette guidelines:

- Review all prereading in advance of the conference.
- Listen attentively.
- List questions and discussion points until there is an opportunity for you to speak.
- State your name and location when you do speak.
- Act just as you would in a face-to-face meeting. Don't let the camera intimidate or distract you. Let yourself get absorbed into the content of the meeting.
- Be aware of what you wear to the video conference. If you think that you may speak at the conference, do not wear distracting colors or patterns. Certain colors, especially white, and patterns (stripes, plaids, small and busy) tend to react adversely to light and may distort the image that is seen by your fellow participants.

So how do you decide which technology to use? Table 3.2, while not all inclusive, may give you a few ideas.

Table 3.2 Communication Technology Reference

Communication	E-mail	Voice Mail	Conference Call	Video Conference
Minutes from a conference call or meeting	X			
Documents for review or response	X			
Discussion	X			
Topic with which the recipients are very familiar and need little explanation	X			

Communication	E-mail	Voice Mail	Conference Call	Video Conference
Date or time-stamped record needed	X			
Desire to provide an opportunity to respond directly in writing	X			
An urgent message needing to be sent during a conference call	X			
Message for a recipient who is out of town or in a meeting with access to a computer	X			
A more personal message		X		
Brainstorm ideas with other virtual team members			X	X
Project status updates			X	
An interview				X
Brief messages that do not require a written record		X		
Significant organizational messages			X	X
An urgent message with some details to an individual who cannot be reached directly		X		
Kick-off for a new virtual team			X	X
Performance appraisal for a distant team member				X

Tips for Improving Productivity

Improving productivity requires a sharp focus on getting more done each day. Set office hours that give you structure while working from home. Plan each work day in advance of beginning to work and set priorities through out the day. Keep a log of work completed each day.

Develop a filing system that works for you. Take breaks every hour or two.

To manage both your work and your time well keep track of deadlines, complete your most difficult tasks first, allocate uninterruptible blocks of time for solo work when you must concentrate, create mini milestones for every task, and batch similar tasks so they can be completed in a single session.

Determine your peak energy times and explore new approaches to complete tasks. Try some of the following techniques.

- Get up early in the morning and go straight to work on your most important task.
- Create a cone of silence once in a while and go to place where you can work without distractions.
- Deliberately pick up the pace, and try to move a little more quickly than usual.
- Take action immediately after setting a goal, even if the action is not perfectly planned.
- Once you have the information you need to make a decision, start a timer and give yourself just sixty seconds to make the actual decision.
- Select a random piece of a larger project, and complete it.
- Identify a new habit you would like to form, and commit to using that habit for at least thirty days.
- Identify the processes you use most often, and write them down step-by-step. Refine them on paper to provide greater efficiency.

- Swap tasks with a colleague who may have certain talents that allow him or her to complete them more quickly than you can.

Avoid the urgency addiction. Urgent tasks are not always the most important. Focus your energy on the critical twenty percent, and don't overengineer the noncritical eighty percent. Visualize your tasks as already completed and give yourself frequent rewards for achievement. Break complex projects into smaller, well-defined tasks. Expand your network outside of your industry to expose you to new ideas.

Use multiple methods of communication. Determine if e-mail, voice mail, conference calls, or video conferences is the most appropriate vehicle to send your message.

4

Maintaining Balance

If you've gotten as far as convincing your manager to modify your schedule to complete at least some of your work from home, congratulations! If you have learned how to set up a productive home office with limited distractions, found some tips to increase your productivity both at your home office and at your company's office, and conquered the technology challenges with both, you may still find an additional struggle not yet touched on—maintaining your work-life balance.

When working from home or even in your organization's office or when doing a little of both, it is far too easy to become unbalanced when it comes to managing your work and personal life. You really have two main things to focus on: your career and all other aspects of your life. Don't sacrifice one for the other. But, rather, keep both in balance (Covey, Merrill, and Merrill 1994).

Learning a work-life balance is imperative when working from home. Take advantage of the flexible schedule, making sufficient time for both work and play. Once you get into the groove, you'll love the benefits of working from your home office.

Take care of yourself and the things that are most important to you as a person. Continue to advance your education, either formally through courses, networking conferences, and reading or informally through self-teaching, learning from others, and reflection. Covey (1990) refers to this as "sharpening the saw," and it is critical to maintaining a sense of balance.

Set Boundaries

Establish a routine for yourself both at work and at play. This does not mean that you can't be spontaneous every so often; spontaneity should be part of your routine. It's healthy to break your routine sometimes, just don't let the break in routine run you over.

Find some "me" time in your routine, and fill it with your ambitions. That could mean taking an art or athletic class, joining a book club, gardening, guest speaking through the local chamber of commerce, volunteering at the local food bank or church, taking up a new sport, or having an afternoon break with friends or neighbors when no business is to be spoken.

Set regular working and playing hours. Communicate these hours to others who live in your home and/or live around you. A visual reminder can help you and others to recognize your schedule. If you have a door leading to your office, close it, post a "Do not disturb" sign or any other significant symbol on your door. If your office does not have a door to close, try a ribbon strung at waist level or a stop sign on a stand at the entrance to your office.

When you have completed your work for the day, shut down your equipment, close the door, don't answer your work phone anymore, and walk away. This is a symbolic way to bring closure to your work day. You not only need to care for your mind but for your physical wellness, which is just as important.

Physical Activity and Nutrition

Covey (1990) has found that physical activity and proper nutrition not only keep you healthy physiologically, they also feed the mind and the soul. The state of your health does dictate how and for how long you should exercise and what your daily nutritional consumption should be. You should discuss these with your physician before taking on a new routine for exercise and nutrition. The recommendations that follow are general examples for a healthy adult.

Regular Physical Activity

Regular physical activity is important for good health, and it's especially important if you're trying to lose weight or maintain a healthy weight. Not only is it good for your weight control, but regular physical activity can reduce the risk of heart attack, stroke, cancer, diabetes, and obesity (Center for Disease Control [CDC] 2009. Physical Activity for Adults, Retrieved on March 3, 2010 from www.cdc.gov/physicalactivity). Physical activity simply means movement of the body that uses energy. Walking, gardening, briskly pushing a baby stroller, climbing the stairs, playing soccer, or dancing the night away are all good examples of being active. For health benefits, physical activity should be moderate or vigorous and add up to at least thirty minutes a day.

Moderate physical activities include:
- walking briskly (about 3.5 miles per hour);
- hiking;
- gardening/yard work;
- dancing;
- golf (walking and carrying clubs);
- bicycling (less than ten miles per hour); and
- weight training (general light workout).

Vigorous physical activities include:
- running/jogging (five miles per hour);
- bicycling (more than ten miles per hour);
- swimming (freestyle laps);
- aerobics;
- walking very fast (4.5 miles per hour);
- heavy yard work, such as chopping wood;

- weight lifting (vigorous effort); and
- basketball (competitive).

Some physical activities are not intense enough to help you meet the recommendations. Although you are moving, these activities do not increase your heart rate, so you should not count these toward the thirty or more minutes per day that you should strive for. These include walking at a casual pace, such as while grocery shopping, and doing light household chores.

According to the 2008 Physical Activity Guidelines for Americans (Center for Disease Control [CDC] 2009. Physical Activity for Adults, Retrieved on March 3, 2010 from www.cdc.gov/physicalactivity), you need to do two types of physical activity each week to improve your health: aerobic and muscle-strengthening. The CDC recommends in those guidelines that adults complete:

- two hours and thirty minutes (150 minutes) of moderate-intensity aerobic activity, such as brisk walking every week and muscle-strengthening activities on two or more days a week that work all major muscle groups (legs, hips, back, abdomen, chest, shoulders, and arms);
- one hour and fifteen minutes (seventy-five minutes) of vigorous-intensity_aerobic activity, such as jogging or running, every week and muscle-strengthening activities on two or more days a week that work all major muscle groups (legs, hips, back, abdomen, chest, shoulders, and arms); or
- an equivalent mix of moderate- and vigorous-intensity aerobic activity and muscle-strengthening activities on two or more days a week that work all major muscle groups (legs, hips, back, abdomen, chest, shoulders, and arms).

You may think 150 minutes each week sounds like a lot of time, but you don't have to do it all at once. Not only is it best to spread your activity out during the week, but you can break it up into smaller chunks of time during the day. As long as you're doing your activity at a moderate or vigorous effort for at least ten minutes at a time.

Aerobic activity or "cardio" gets you breathing harder and your heart beating faster. From pushing a lawn mower to taking a dance class to biking to the store—all types of activities count, as long as you're doing them at a moderate or vigorous intensity for at least ten minutes at a time.

Intensity is how hard your body is working during aerobic activity. With moderate-intensity aerobic activity, you're working hard enough to raise your heart rate and break a sweat. One way to tell is that you'll be able to talk but not sing the words to your favorite song. Build up over time. If you want to do more vigorous-level activities, slowly replace those that take moderate effort, like brisk walking, with more vigorous activities, like jogging. With vigorous-intensity aerobic activity, you're breathing hard and fast, and your heart rate has gone up quite a bit. If you're working at this level, you won't be able to say more than a few words without pausing for a breath.

You can do moderate- or vigorous-intensity aerobic activity, or a mix of the two, each week. A rule of thumb is that one minute of vigorous-intensity activity is about the same as two minutes of moderate-intensity activity (Dr. Wayne Tucker 2006, personal communication). Some people like to do vigorous types of activity because it gives them about the same health benefits in half the time. If you haven't been very active lately, increase your activity level slowly. You need to feel comfortable doing moderate-intensity activities before you move on to more vigorous ones. The guidelines emphasize doing physical activity that is right for you.

Along with aerobic activity, strengthen your muscles at least two days a week. These activities should work all the major muscle groups of your body (legs, hips, back, chest, abdomen, shoulders, and arms). To gain health benefits, muscle-strengthening activities need to be done to the point where it's hard for you to do another repetition without help. A repetition is one complete movement of an activity, like lifting a weight or doing a sit-up. Try to do eight to twelve repetitions per activity; that counts as one set. Try to do at least one set of muscle-strengthening activities, but to gain even more benefits, do two or three sets.

You can do activities that strengthen your muscles on the same days or on different days than when you do aerobic activity—whatever works best. Just keep in mind that muscle-strengthening activities don't count toward your aerobic activity total.

There are many ways you can strengthen your muscles, whether at home or in the gym. You may want to try:

- lifting weights;
- working with resistance bands;
- doing exercises that use your body weight for resistance (i.e., push-ups, sit-ups);
- heavy gardening (i.e., digging, shoveling); or
- yoga.

Not only is physical activity important for your mental and physical well-being, what you eat is critical as well.

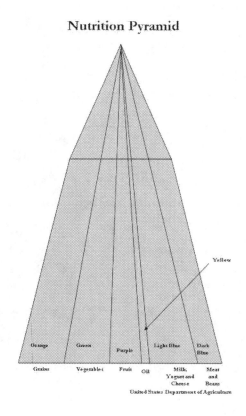

Nutrition Pyramid

Nutrition

Nutrition is critical to your overall health. Making healthy choices in menu selection is easy when you use the nutrition pyramid. The following recommendations are provided by the Nutrition Council of the United States Department of Agriculture (USDA 2010 Find Healthy Eating Choices, retrieved on line March 10, 2010 from www. nutrition.gov) in the color-coded nutrition pyramid:

- **Orange (Grains)** – many foods made from wheat, rice, oats, cornmeal, barley, or another cereal grain are grain products. Bread, pasta, oatmeal, breakfast cereals, tortillas, and grits are examples of grain products. Grains are divided into two subgroups: whole grains and refined grains.
- Whole grains contain the entire grain kernel—the bran, the germ, and the endosperm.
- Refined grains have been milled, a process that removes the bran and the germ. This is done to give grains a finer texture and improve their shelf life, but it also removes dietary fiber, iron, and many B vitamins. Most refined grains are enriched. This means certain B vitamins (thiamin, riboflavin, niacin, folic acid) and iron are added back in after processing. Fiber is not added back in to enriched grains. Check the ingredient list on refined grain products to make sure that the word "enriched" is included in the grain name.
- Some food products are made from mixtures of whole grains and refined grains. Check the ingredient list for the words "whole grain" or "whole wheat" to decide if they are made from a whole grain.
- Some grain products contain significant amounts of bran. Bran provides fiber, which is important for health. However, products with added bran or bran alone (e.g., oat bran) are not necessarily whole grain products.

- **Green** – Any vegetable or 100 percent vegetable juice counts as a member of the vegetable group. Vegetables may be raw or cooked; fresh, frozen, canned, or dried/dehydrated; and may be whole, cut up, or mashed. Vegetables are organized into five subgroups, based on their nutrient content: dark green, orange, dry beans and peas, starchy, and other.
- **Purple** – Any fruit or 100 percent fruit juice counts toward this food group. Fruits can be fresh, canned, frozen or dried, whole, cut up, or pureed. You should eat a variety of fruits.
- **Yellow** – Oils come from many different plants and from fish. Some oils are used mainly as flavorings, such as walnut oil and sesame oil. A number of foods are naturally high in oils.
- Oils are fats that are liquid at room temperature, like the vegetable oils used in cooking. Most oils are high in monounsaturated or polyunsaturated fats, and low in saturated fats. Oils from plant sources (vegetable and nut oils) do not contain any cholesterol. In fact, no foods from plants sources contain cholesterol.
- A few plant oils, however—including coconut oil and palm kernel oil—are high in saturated fats and, for nutritional purposes, should be considered to be solid fats. Solid fats are fats that are solid at room temperature, like butter and shortening. Solid fats come from many animal foods and can be made from vegetable oils through a process called hydrogenation.
- **Light Blue** – All fluid milk products and many foods that are made from milk are considered part of this food group. Foods made from milk that retain their calcium content are part of the group, while foods made from milk that have little to no calcium, such as cream cheese, cream, and

butter, are not. Most milk group choices should be fat-free or low-fat.

- **Dark Blue** – All foods made from meat, poultry, fish, dry beans or peas, eggs, nuts, and seeds are considered part of this group since they contain measurable levels of protein, vitamins, and minerals. Dry beans and peas are part of this group as well as the vegetable group. Most meat and poultry choices should be lean or low-fat. Fish, nuts, and seeds contain healthy oils, so choose these foods frequently instead of meat or poultry.

Table 4.1 lists commonly eaten foods in each category, and the USDA-recommended consumption amounts based on healthy adults who exercise for thirty minutes per day.

Table 4.1 Healthy Eating with the Nutrition Pyramid

Food Group	Orange (Grains)				
Subcategories	Whole Grains	Refined Grains			
	• brown rice • buckwheat • bulgur • oatmeal • popcorn • whole wheat cereal flakes • muesli • whole grain barley • whole grain cornmeal • whole rye • whole wheat bread • whole wheat crackers • whole wheat pasta • whole wheat buns/rolls • whole wheat tortillas • wild rice • amaranth • millet • quinoa • sorghum • triticale	• cornbread • corn tortillas • couscous • crackers • flour tortillas • grits • noodles • spaghetti • macaroni • pitas • pretzels			

USDA Recommended Amounts					
Men, all ages	At least 1.5 ounces per day	At least 1.5 ounces per day			
Women, all ages	At least 1.5 ounces per day	At least 1.5 ounces per day			

Food Group			Green (Vegetables)		
Subcategories	Dark Green	Orange	Dry Beans and Peas	Starchy Vegetables	Other Vegetables
	• bok choy • broccoli • collard greens • dark green, leafy lettuce • kale • mesclun • mustard greens • romaine lettuce • spinach • turnip greens • watercress	• acorn squash • butternut squash • carrots • Hubbard squash • pumpkin • sweet potatoes	• black beans • black-eyed peas • garbanzo beans (chick peas) • kidney beans • lentils • lima beans (mature) • navy beans • pinto beans • soybeans • split peas • tofu (bean curd from soy beans) • white beans	• corn • green peas • lima beans (green) • potatoes	• artichokes • asparagus • bean sprouts • beets • brussels sprouts • cabbage • cauliflower • celery • cucumbers • eggplant • green and wax beans • green or red peppers • iceberg lettuce • mushrooms • okra • onions • parsnips • tomatoes • vegetable juices • turnips • zucchini
USDA Recommended Amounts					
Men, age 19-50	3 cups per week	2 cups per week	3 cups per week	6 cups per week	7 cups per week
Men, age 51+	3 cups per week	2 cups per week	3 cups per week	3 cups per week	6.5 cups per week
Women, age 19-50	3 cups per week	2 cups per week	3 cups per week	3 cups per week	6.5 cups per week
Women, age 50+	2 cups per week	1.5 cups per week	2.5 cups per week	2.5 cups per week	5.5 cups per week

Food Group	Purple (Fruit)					
Subcategories	• apples • raspberries • lemons • watermelon • pears • raisins	• apricots • cherries • limes • fruit cocktail • papaya	• tangerines • avocado • grapefruit • mangoes • nectarines	• pineapple • 100 percent orange juice • bananas • grapes • cantaloupe	• oranges • plums • 100 percent apple juice • strawberries • kiwi fruit	• honeydew • peaches • prunes • 100 percent grape juice • 100 percent grapefruit juice
USDA Recommended Amounts						
Men, all ages	2 cups per day					
Women, age 19-30	2 cups per day					
Women, age 31+	1.5 cups per day					

Food Group	Yellow (Oils)	
Subcategories	Oils	Solid Fats
	• canola • corn • cottonseed • olive • safflower • soybean • sunflower	• butter • beef fat • chicken fat • pork fat • stick margarine • shortening
USDA Recommended Amounts		
Men, age 19-30	7 teaspoons per day	
Men, age 31+	6 teaspoons per day	
Women, age 19-30	6 teaspoons per day	
Women, age 31+	5 teaspoons per day	

Food Group	Light Blue (Milk, Yogurt, and Cheese)			
Subcategories	Milk	Milk-Based Desserts	Cheese	Yogurt
	• fat-free milk (skim) • low-fat milk (1%) • reduced-fat milk (2%) • chocolate milk • strawberry milk • lactose-free milk	• pudding made with milk • ice milk • frozen yogurt • ice cream	• cheddar • mozzarella • Swiss • parmesan • ricotta cheese • cottage cheese • American	• fat-free • low-fat • reduced-fat • whole-milk
USDA Recommended Amounts				
Men, all ages	3 cups per day			
Women, all ages	3 cups per day			

Food Group Subcategories	Dark Blue (Meat, Poultry, Fish, and Beans)					
	Meat	Poultry	Eggs	Dry Beans and Peas	Nuts and Seeds	Fish
	• beef • ham • lamb • pork • veal • bison • rabbit • venison • lean luncheon meats • liver • giblets	• chicken • duck • goose • turkey	• chicken eggs • duck eggs	• black beans • black-eyed peas • garbanzo, kidney beans • falafel • lentils • lima beans (mature) • navy, white beans • pinto beans • soy beans • split peas • tofu • garden burgers • veggie burgers • textured vegetable protein (TVP)	• almonds • cashews • hazelnuts • mixed nuts • peanuts • peanut butter • pecans • pistachios • pumpkin seeds • sesame seeds • sunflower seeds • walnuts	• catfish • flounder, haddock, cod • halibut • herring, mackerel • pollock • porgy • salmon, tuna • sea bass, trout • snapper • swordfish • clams, mussels, oysters • crab, scallops, lobster • crayfish, shrimp • oysters, squid, octopus • anchovies, sardines
USDA Recommended Amounts						
Men, age 19-30	6.5 ounces per day					
Men, age 31-50	6 ounces per day					
Men, age 50+	5.5 ounces per day					
Women, age 19-30	5.5 ounces per day					
Women, age 31+	5 ounces per day					

Source: United States Department of Agriculture (2010) www.nutrition.gov

Reistad-Long (2010 Chow down on eats that tame hunger and reduce anxiety. Retrieved on line March 24, 2010 from www.health.yahoo.com/featured/87/8-foods-that-fight-stress) lists eight foods that fight stress. They include:

1. Dark chocolate is high in flavonoids that are known for their relaxing properties. Chocolate also contains phenylethylamine, a chemical that enhances your mood. The darker the chocolate, the more healthy substances you're getting in your diet, so look for bars that are 70 percent cacao or higher.

2. Low-fat milk is calming when warm. One study found that women who drank four or more servings of low-fat milk every day were about half as likely to experience stress-related symptoms as those who drank less than one serving per week.

3. Oatmeal contains carbohydrates that help you produce serotonin, a calming hormone that helps fight anxiety's negative effects—which is probably why you may crave carbohydrates when you're stressed out. Oatmeal is high in fiber, which means that your body will absorb it slowly. In one fell swoop, you'll prolong the serotonin boost, keeping yourself feeling full for longer (and on less) and making sure your blood sugar is in check.

4. Salmon contains omega-3 fatty acids that can help reverse stress symptoms by boosting serotonin levels. An omega-3–rich diet can also help suppress the production of the anxiety hormones cortisol and adrenaline.

5. Walnuts have been shown to lower blood pressure, which is critical for those whose hearts are already working overtime, thanks to high adrenaline levels. In fact, research so strongly backs the health benefits of walnuts that the United States Food and Drug Administration goes as far as to recommend 1.5 ounces per day.

6. Sunflower seeds provide a good source of folate, which in turn helps your body produce a pleasure-inducing brain chemical called dopamine.

7. Spinach and other leafy greens are abundant in magnesium, improve your body's response to stress.

8. Blueberries contain antioxidants that counteract the effects of stress hormones, like cortisol and adrenaline, on your body.

Not only can physical activity and good nutrition reduce stress-related symptoms, but there are many other ways to manage your stress levels.

Managing Stress

Stress has the potential of exerting unwanted influence on a person's susceptibility to various illnesses. It can also speed up the progress of illness and disease, ranging from the common cold to cancer. There is a link between one's evolutionary process and one's bodily reaction to stress. In primitive times, human beings were constantly threatened by their environment and faced physical threats from animals and nature. Human beings have learned to cope with physical stress. The heart pumps blood faster, and the body prepares to face any forthcoming challenges. The fight-or-flight response, triggered by the release of adrenaline, is also a part of one's evolutionary process (Segal 2001).

The problem arises when the body is prepared for yet incapable of facing its perils. For example, if you are stuck in a traffic jam, a fight-or-flight response is of no use; there is nothing you can do. This causes your blood pressure to rise, and you may possibly lose your cool, but it is all needless as the situation is beyond your control. The unnecessary rise of blood pressure is an example of a stress-related illness. It is actually an accumulation of frustration (Segal 2001).

There are various other determinants of stress-related illnesses. Scientists have investigated behavior-oriented stress disorders. They have classified people into various types. A type A person is one of those people who are highly competitive and have a certain drive. He or she is an ambitious person who is ready to give it his or her heart and soul. Such people are goal-oriented and highly focused. Type A people are also known as workaholics and are always subjected to stress (Koss 2009).

On the other hand, there are people who have hardly any focus in life, who may be unemployed or just plain complacent. They, too, can be equally prone to stress. It is actually a matter of resilience. Stress-related disorders are very subjective, because people have various levels of stress tolerance. When the stress overpowers the tolerance level, stress-related disorders are imminent (Koss 2009).

Numerous surveys and studies confirm that occupational pressures and fears are far and away the leading source of stress for American adults and that these have steadily increased over the past few decades. While there are many statistics to support these findings, the significance depends on how the information was obtained (self-reported versus answers to carefully worded questions), the size and demographics of the target group, how participants were selected, and who sponsored the study. Some self-serving polls claiming that a particular occupation is "the most stressful" are conducted by unions or organizations in an attempt to get higher wages or better benefits for their members. Others may be conducted to promote a product, such as the Stress in the Nineties survey by the maker of a deodorant that found housewives were under more stress than the CEOs of major corporations. Such a conclusion might be anticipated since telephone calls to residential phones were conducted in the afternoon (Koss 2009). It is crucial to keep all these caveats in mind when evaluating job stress statistics. The National Institute of Stress and Health (NIOSH) is an excellent resource that cites the following statistics from the 1990s:

- 40 percent of workers reported that their jobs were very or extremely stressful.

- 25 percent viewed their jobs as the number one stressor in their lives.
- 75 percent of employees believed that workers have more on-the-job stress than a generation before.
- 29 percent of employees felt quite a bit or extremely stressed at work.
- 26 percent of employees said they were "often or very often burned out or stressed by their work."
- Job stress is more strongly associated with health complaints than financial or family problems are.

This information was obtained through large surveys by Northwestern National Life Insurance Company, Princeton Survey Research Associates, St. Paul Fire and Marine Insurance Company, Yale University, and the Families and Work Institute.

More recently, the 2001 annual "Attitudes in the American Workplace VI" Gallup Poll sponsored by the Marlin Company (www. Gallup.com/globalattitudesandbehaviors/2001) found that:

- 80 percent of employees felt stress on the job;
- 49 percent said they needed help in learning how to manage stress;
- 42 percent said their coworkers needed such help ;
- 14 percent of respondents had felt like striking a coworker in the past year, but hadn't;
- 25 percent had felt like screaming or shouting because of job stress;
- 10 percent were concerned about an individual at work who they fear could become violent;
- 9 percent were aware of an assault or violent act in their workplace; and
- 18 percent had experienced some sort of threat or verbal intimidation in the past year.

Cottrell and Harvey (2005) conducted a survey to determine what caused employee stress. They found that most employees create their own stress by worrying about many things that not only are insignificant, but were also mostly issues or situations beyond their reasonable control:

- 40 percent of the worries concerned things that did not actually happen;
- 30 percent of the worries concerned things in the past that could not be changed nor otherwise influenced;
- 12 percent were needless worries about health;
- 10 percent were petty unimportant worries;
- 8 percent of the worries concerned something substantial; and
- 4 percent of the substantial worries involved things that could be controlled and/or changed.

The best antidote for worry is action; do whatever you can to minimize the chances that what you fear will actually happen. Through action, you free yourself from the victim mentality that can paralyze even the best employees. Additionally, get the facts. Most worry is based on false assumptions. Get the real facts, and don't let your energy be drained by invalid or unsubstantiated concerns.

Think about the worst case scenario. You may discover that situations are not as bad as you originally thought. Understanding the legitimate ramifications of issues helps you put them in perspective. And, it cuts down on the number of concerns that compete for your attention.

Try to improve the potential negative outcomes of legitimate concerns. Then, if you've done everything you can to prevent the worry from being realized, let it go. Focus your energy and attention on other issues. Excessive worrying is counterproductive. It's an unnecessary waste of energy and emotion, and it may make you miserable.

Keep an optimistic outlook by surrounding yourself with positive people. Negative people can destroy morale. One negative person can influence scores of others. A negative person has a far greater influence on others than a positive, optimistic person does (Cottrell and Harvey 2005). Negative people can drain energy, destroy confidence, create conflict, hamper innovation and initiative, and reduce overall productivity in others.

Another way to keep an optimistic outlook is to create a customized, stress-free workspace. Think about the most relaxing places you know of. What is it about those places that make you feel good? What are the sights, sounds, and smells? How can you modify your workspace to create a similar feel? You might not be able to duplicate the feeling perfectly, but you can always get close. If you don't have time for a complete workspace makeover, then just make one little change each week.

Most likely, you'll use your chair more than you will any other object in your workspace, so consider investing in a good one. Today, there is an assortment of oddities you can sit on, including knee chairs, balls, and more. Visit an office supply store and find something that suits you. If your company won't allow you to expense a high-quality office chair, then consider buying your own. Purchase an ergonomically correct chair, and adding a back massager to it.

Must a professional workspace be a sterile sea of beige and gray to be productive? Remember that where you work you also live. Given the amount of time you'll be living in your workspace over the course of your lifetime, it makes sense to add some visual appeal (eHow 2008). Paint your office your favorite color. Make sure it is soothing, however, and not something you will tire of easily. Paint is one of the least expensive and easiest ways to transform a room.

The first time you see your workspace each day, you should feel good about it. It should be attractive to you. It should be your favorite place in the entire building or house. If you're in your workspace right now, please step outside for a minute and then reenter it while paying close attention to your sense impressions. What's the first emotional response you can detect? Do you feel stressed? Overwhelmed? Bored? Apathetic? Focused? Peaceful? Is this an emotion you experience often while working?

Now choose the emotion you want to feel and experiment with different visual elements to see how they alter your feelings. Try new furniture, photos, posters, mirrors, flowers, knick knacks, toys, statues, rugs, artwork, crystals, etc. If you have the necessary control, you can also tweak the lighting in your workspace to create the right mood. You may know a programmer who works in a completely dark room with no windows and loves it (Allen 2002).

Does your workspace look like an automaton works there, or does it include elements that are uniquely you? Remember that your workspace is your living space for much of your day, so make it livable and not just workable. A good way to accomplish this is by adding items that hold emotional significance for you. Photographs, prints, sentimental plaques and paintings are easy ways to personalize your space.

One look at a cluttered workspace and you get a sense that the person working there is stressed, overwhelmed, and disorganized. Most managers will not promote a person with a messy workspace into a position of responsibility. It's assumed that if you can't organize your physical environment, you're probably incompetent to a certain degree and can't be trusted. And if layoffs happen, you can imagine who the most obvious targets are. Clear the clutter from your workspace. Even more critical is the effect a cluttered workspace has on your focus. It's difficult to feel centered when you're surrounded by unfinished tasks that constantly remind you of what you haven't done yet. Ideally, the only paper items on your desk should be directly related to the current task at hand. Store everything else in drawers, shelves, or cabinets. Many people notice a dramatic improvement in their productivity when they employ this strategy (eHow 2008 Make money from home, retrieved on line February 22, 2010 from www.chow.com/how_5936906 -make-money-stay-home).

Plants are a wonderful way to add life to a lifeless workspace. You want to create positive energy in your work environment. Use only living, oxygen-generating plants, not lifeless, artificial ones. Water them as needed to keep them healthy. Over time, you'll find that your plants begin to resonate with you and become a reflection of you. Dying plants equal a dead career. Artificial plants equate with "appears successful but empty on the inside." Healthy plants equal healthy career. A lot of plants equals abundance. Bring yourself back to nature by adding some plants to your workspace, and you'll find yourself enjoying the environment much more.

Make your office smell good. Australian dentist Paddy Lund has his staff bake fresh muffins for his patients daily. Think about how a dentist's office usually smells. Now imagine walking into one that smells of blueberry muffins. Along with other changes, this reportedly helped Lund increase his income by a factor of ten (Editors of Consumer Reports Books 2008). This is not to suggest you add a Holly Hobby Easy-Bake Oven to your workspace, but there are plenty of practical ways to make it smell better than cleaning supplies.

Certain scents have a measurable effect on productivity, especially lemon and lavender (Editors of Consumer Reports Books 2008). Not only do scented candles, especially the three-inch by six-inch pillars, make your office smell good, but the colorful candles and decorative candle holders add visual appeal as well. If you don't like candles, there are other options for improving the smell of your office. You can get a diffuser and fill it with essential oil, add some potpourri, or even try sliced lemons. Be careful when considering chemical air fresheners though, as there are reports that they can pose health risks.

Experiment with different types of music to see what effect they have on your stress level and productivity. Use headphones if you need to keep from disturbing others. You may prefer total silence when you do certain types of work, and some like listening to music while completing routine tasks.

Even with good air conditioning, you might have periods when you just want to feel a little cooler, or maybe you'd like a bit of air circulation. Use a small portable fan to keep your comfort level right where you want it to be.

If you find the sounds of running water soothing, consider adding a small fountain to your workspace. You can get a basic one for less than twenty dollars. You may even add an illuminated rock garden fountain to the corner of your office. Plug the power supply into the same power base you use for your PC equipment, so you can simply flip a switch in front of you to turn it on. If you do add a fountain, remember to add water to it every few days. This may help remind you to water your plants as well.

Negotiate for a period of time each day when you turn off all outside communication, and encase yourself in a cocoon of concentration. Put up a "Do not disturb" sign, turn off your phone, disable your instant messenger, and don't check e-mail either. Use this time to work on the tasks that cause you the greatest stress or which require your utmost concentration. It's easier to relax and focus when you know you won't be interrupted. Some jobs obviously require more solo concentration time than others—a computer programmer may need a lot, while a receptionist may need virtually none. Determine how much you need to be productive, and do whatever is necessary to get it.

Take a moment to survey your workspace and jot down a few changes you'd like to make. How can you make your workspace even more relaxing, livable, and attractive? If cash is tight, set a budget for how much you'd like to spend on making your workspace stress free. Maybe your employer will pay for some of it, especially if it's likely to boost your productivity.

Mind Like Water, a book written by Jim Ballard (2002), offers busy people a set of specific tools for maintaining a state of balance and perspective from which to respond to changing events. "Mind like water" is a way to get a grip on it all, stay relaxed, and get meaningful things done with minimal effort—across the whole spectrum of your work and life. You can experience what the martial artists call "mind like water" and the athletes call "the zone," within the complex world in which you are engaged (Allen 2002). You may have been there from time to time. It's a condition of working, doing, and being in which the mind is clear and constructive things are happening. It is accessible to everyone and is increasingly needed to deal with the complex world of this century. More and more, it will become a required condition for high-performing professionals who wish to maintain balance and a consistent, positive output in their work.

In karate there is an image used to explain perfect readiness, or "mind like water." Imagine tossing a pebble into a still pond. How does the water react? The water reacts appropriately to the force and mass of the input and then it returns to calm. It doesn't overreact or underreact. The power of a karate punch comes from speed, not muscle; it comes from the *pop* at the end of the whip. That's why petite people can break boards and bricks with their hands. It doesn't take calluses or brute strength, just the ability to generate a focused thrust with speed. But a tense muscle is a slow one.

The high levels of training in the martial arts teach balance and relaxation as much as anything else. Clearing the mind and flexibility are keys (Allen 2002). Anything that causes you to overreact or underreact can control you. Responding inappropriately to colleagues, family, your manager, e-mails, unread magazines, or thoughts about uncompleted tasks can lead to less effective results than you desire. Most people give either more or less attention to things than is required, simply because they do not operate with a mind like water.

Practice stress-relieving activities. There are several short, simple things you can do to relieve stress throughout the day. For each of the following exercises, stand leaning forward in the ready position and maintain a deep, easy breathing pattern throughout.

- Breathe through the diaphragm.
  1. Place your hands on your lower rib cage.
  2. Inhale deeply through your nose. The expansion you feel in your lower rib cage is caused by your diaphragm muscle expanding and dropping as the air pushes against it. Your shoulders should not move.

3. Exhale, allowing the air to slowly escape through your slightly open mouth. You will feel a depression around your lower rib cage as the diaphragm rises like a trampoline to support and propel the air.

4. Repeat these steps several times until you find your rhythm, when breathing is effortless. There should be a feeling of being calm yet full of energy.

5. Do the exercise one more time, moving one hand from the side of your lower rib cage to your abdomen. When you inhale, your breath should push your hand away from the abdominal area. If this does not happen, you are not breathing deeply enough for the diaphragm to do its job.

6. Remember that, while inhaling, the abdominal area should fill up first and more fully than your chest.

- Tone and relax your head and neck.
  1. Relax your jaw so your mouth is slightly open.
  2. Slowly drop (don't push) your head to your chest and then bring it back to the center. Drop your head to your left shoulder and then back to center. Drop your head to your right shoulder and then back to center.
  3. Beginning at center, do two head rolls to the right. Return to center and do two head rolls to the left.
  4. Monitor your breathing throughout the exercise; make sure you are not holding your breath. Keep your jaw loose.

- Tone and relax your shoulders.
  1. With your hands at your sides, clench your fists.
  2. Lift your shoulders as close to your ears as you can.
  3. Drop your shoulders and release your fists with a thrust, sighing as you exhale.
  4. Do six slow shoulder rolls to the back, keeping your jaw loose. Feel your chest expand, sigh as you exhale.
  5. Do six slow shoulder rolls to the front; sigh as you exhale.

- Tone and relax your face.
  1. Make the tiniest face you can. Pucker your lips, close your eyes, and tighten your muscles.
  2. Open into the widest face you make.
  3. Return to the tight position and try to move your entire face to the right-hand side. Then try to move your face to the left-hand side.
  4. Return to the wide position and repeat the exercise.
- Tone and relax your lips.
  1. Take a deep breath.
  2. Pucker your lips.
  3. As you exhale, force the air through your puckered lips. This will result in a *brr* sound and will direct vibrating energy to your lips while relaxing them.

These exercises may make you a little uncomfortable in front of other people. If so, try them in a private place.

When you are having a high anxiety moment, take a walk, preferably in one of your favorite, peaceful places. Reflect on that difficult project or whatever the main stressors of that day are and choose to center your mind on the main cause of your anxiety. Within ten minutes, you can feel refreshed again and energized enough to conquer those taxing issue(s) (Morrow Lindbergh 1991).

As you have read, there's a whole lot of stress going on. Learn the work-life balance that is imperative when working from home.

Key Tips for Maintaining Balance

Learning the work-life balance is imperative when working from home. Take advantage of the flexible schedule, making sufficient time for both working and playing. You have two main things to focus on---one for your work and another for all the other aspects of your life. Don't sacrifice one for the other. But rather, keep both in balance (Covey, Merrill and Merrill 1994).

Establish a routine for your self both at work and at play. Be spontaneous once in while. Find time in your routine to fulfill your ambitions.

Set regular working and playing hours. Communicate these hours to others who live in your home and around your home. When you have completed your work for the day, shut down your office and walk away.

Covey (1990) found that physical activity and proper nutrition not only keep you healthy physiologically, but they also feed the mind and the soul. The state of your health does dictate how you should exercise, for how long, and what your daily nutritional consumption should be. Discuss these with your physician before taking on new routine for exercise and nutrition.

Maintaining balance includes keeping your stress in control. Stress has the potential of exerting unwanted influence on a person's susceptibility to various illnesses from the common cold to cancer and stroke. Try some of the following techniques along with healthy exercise and nutrition.

- design your workspace in a way that relieves stress;
- plan a period of time each day when you can turn off all outside communication, and encase yourself in a cocoon of concentration; and,
- practice stress relieving exercises everyday.

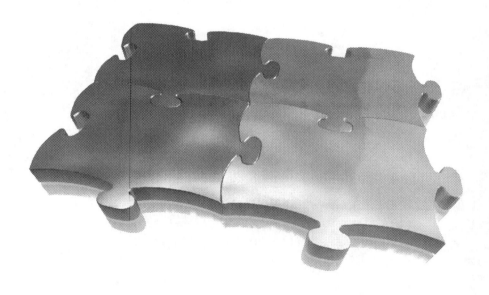

5

Putting It All Together

In today's volatile economy, companies are looking for ways to reduce costs and increase revenues. In turn, they are looking to employees for solutions. Heskett, Sasser, and Schlesinger (1997) interpreted this shift in corporate executives' thinking as the service profit chain. The philosophy of this model is that when employees are enabled—through accessible tools, resources, training, teamwork, adequate working conditions, respect, and control—to perform their jobs successfully, customer satisfaction improves, leading to greater customer loyalty and, eventually, increased profits. Employees thrive on challenges and variety in their tasks and environments. Lack of control often leads to stress for employees and can lead to a number of stress-related illnesses, such as colds, headaches, strokes, cancer, and heart attacks.

What factors cause employees stress? Although many things can cause stress, the leading factors include the commute to the job site, the distractions at work, and the rigid and stressful daily routine (Allen 2001). Employees often believe that they have no control over any of these things. But, the truth is that today's employees can have control over these variables and, at the same time, increase their company's bottom line.

Working from home spares the company certain expenses and increases the company's profitability through improved productivity. Through some creativity and ingenuity, employees can create a work life that includes an improved state of mind, body, and health by working from home even just one or two days a week; employers save money and gain a happy employee who can be even more productive. It's a win-win situation.

Some jobs must be performed on an organization's premises. However, many jobs can be successfully performed from home, either part- or full-time. Employees can easily sort through the tasks required in their jobs and determine if there are some that, when grouped together, could be successfully completed remotely (at a home office). However, working from home takes discipline, so it may not be the right fit for everyone.

Working from home is being embraced by more employees and employers every day. Being close to family, eliminating a commute, and setting one's own schedule is a wonderful way to work and enjoy life at the same time. Employees who choose to work from home must be very dedicated to producing a certain amount of work every day as well as committed to a set of rules that they create for themselves and their companies. Even though employees are working alone from home, they can still be expert virtual team members with a little study and practice.

Are you tired of commuting to the office every day and dealing with the same office politics? Are the rising costs of gas, food, and clothing taking a toll on your personal finances? Wouldn't it be great to pour a cup of coffee or tea in the kitchen, sit down in your home office, and start working as soon as you awaken? Employees desiring to work from home must determine if it is a good fit for them and the organization by considering:

- How strong is the desire to work from home?
- How important are work place relationships for you?
- Can you adapt to doing everything without an assistant?

- Do you consider yourself to be an organized person? Organized people can often get more done without office distractions.
- Do you love what you do? People who love what they do are less likely to procrastinate.
- Is there adequate space in the home to designate a space for working only?
- Do you have support from others living in the household is necessary.

The first obstacle that may need to be overcome is that of convincing the manager that some work from home can be beneficial for both the company and the employee. Some people embrace an older stereotype of working, based on their past experiences and living in a traditional culture. They believe that work only gets done at the organization's facility. While this is undoubtedly true for some jobs, there are many jobs with tasks that can be successfully completed remotely. The discussion with the manager about working from home must be carefully planned and deliberately carried out.

Planning your discussion with your manager requires preparation to make the case, including a thorough analysis of the job to sort out which tasks can be accomplished remotely and which tasks must be completed on the premises. It is critical to share facts and figures with the manager to illustrate how the company and the employee can benefit with alternative work schedules. Once the planning is complete, the employee needs to schedule a one-on-one meeting with the manager. Timing and location for this meeting are very important. A thirty-minute meeting when the manager can dedicate full attention to the employee in the manager's office is probably the best choice.

Delivering a powerful and persuasive argument takes effective communication to demonstrate confidence and believability. The nine key communication behaviors should be practiced and polished to deliver a confident and persuasive message. Those skills are:

- eye communication;
- posture;
- gestures and facial expressions;
- dress and appearance;
- voice and vocal variety;
- language, pauses, and nonwords;
- listener involvement;
- humor; and
- be natural.

Being successful at working from home takes dedicating an adequate space solely for working and nothing else, proper equipment and supplies, a separation between work life and home life, and a routine for working at home similar to the routine for working at the company's office.

Improving productivity while working in a home office can be accomplished by developing a few good habits. Work-at-home employees should learn to plan and prioritize goals each day, keep a log of accomplishments, and share them with the manager and coworkers each week. They should develop a proper filing system from the onset, take frequent breaks, reduce home distractions, and focus on the most important tasks each day and complete them. In addition, using technology appropriately (i.e., e-mail, voice mail, conference calls, webcasts, video conferences) can enhance productivity.

Employees need to maintain a healthy work-life balance. This can be accomplished by setting boundaries for work, family, and play time. They should take care of themselves physically by participating in regular aerobic/cardio and muscle-strengthening exercise and by nourishing the body with a healthy diet aligned with the USDA's nutrition pyramid.

Even though working from home can greatly reduce many of the typical stresses stemming from work, like anything else, a few new or unexpected stresses may arise from your new work lifestyle. Manage stress by maintaining a positive outlook and by surrounding yourself with others who are optimistic. Create a relaxing work space that suits you and practice stress-relieving activities every day. If you ever feel an anxiety attack coming on, take a walk or think of the most relaxing place to be. Remember the principles of mind like water.

Learning the work-life balance is imperative when working from home. Take advantage of the flexible schedule, making sufficient time for both work and play. Once you get into the groove, you will love the benefits of working from home!

References

Allen, David. 2002. Getting Things Done: The Art of Stress Free Productivity. London: Penguin.

Ballard, Jim. 2002. Keeping Your Balance in a Chaotic World, New York: Wiley.

Benson, Laurie K. 2000. Manager's Pocket Guide to eCommunication: Communicating Effectively in a Digital Age. Amherst: Human Resource Development Press.

Buckingham, Marcus and Curt Coffman. 1999. First, Break All the Rules: What the World's Greatest Managers Do Differently. New York: Simon & Schuster.

Childress, John R. and Larry E. Senn. 1995. In the Eye of the Storm: Re-Engineering Corporate Culture. Los Angeles: Leadership Press.

Churchard, Claire. Job cuts needn't harm employee performance. Paper presented online at CybErg 96 Virtual Conference, April 21, 2009. http://www.peoplemanagement.co.uk/pm/articles /2009/04/job-cuts-neednt-harm-performance-argues-think-tank-chief.htm.

Conrad-Stoppler, M. 2007. Stress and your health. *Medecinenet* 74:1;12-17.

Cottrell, David and Eric Harvey. 2005. Leadership Courage. Flower Mound, TX: Walk the Talk Company.

Cottrell, David, Ken Carnes, and Mark C. Layton. 2003. Management Insights. New York: Cornertone Leadership Institute.

Covey, Stephen R. 1990. The 7 Habits of Highly Effective People. New York: Fireside.

Covey, Stephen R., A. Roger Merrill, and Rebecca R. Merrill. 1994. First Things First. New York: Simon & Schuster.

Current Employment Statistics. Bureau of Labor Statistics. http://bls.gov/ces.

Decker, Bert. 1996. The Art of Communicating. Menlo Park, CA: Crisp Publications.

Dilworth, Robert L, and Verna J. Willis. 2003 Action Learning: Images and Pathways. Malabar, FL: Krieger Publishing Company.

Editors of Consumer Reports Books (eds.). 2008. The New Medicine Show: Consumers Union's Practical Guide to Some Everyday Health Problems and Health Products. Consumer Reports Books: Mount Vernon, VA.

Heskett, James L., W. Earl Sasser Jr, and Leonard A. Schlesinger. 1997. The Service Profit Chain. New York: The Free Press.

Kaye, Beverly L. 1997. Up Is Not the Only Way: A Guide to Developing Workforce Talent, Second Edition. Palo Alto, CA: Davies-Black Publishing.

Kaye, Beverly L. and Susan Jordan-Evans. 2008. Love 'Em or Lose 'Em. San Francisco: Berrett-Kohler Publishers.

Koss, B. 2009. The conference call groove. *Chicago Tribune*, March 24, Business section.

Make money from home. eHow. http://www.ehow.com/how_5936906_make-money-stay-home.html.

Mayer, M. 2002. Virtual Leadership: Secrets from the Round Table. Amherst: Human Resources Development.

Mehrabian, Albert. 1992. Silent Messages. Belmont, CA: Wadsworth Publishing Company.

Meredith, J. The fourth generation of time management. Champions Club Community. http://covey.championsclubcommunity.com /2009/07/12/four-generations-of-time-management/.

Morrow Lindbergh, Anne. 1991. Gift from the Sea. New York: Pantheon Books.

Palavino, S. Productivity in the workplace. Bureau of Labor Statistics. http://www.bls.gov/bls/productivity.htm.

Physical Activity for Adults. Center for Disease Control. www.cdc.gov/physicalactivity.

Productivity Improvement. Accel-Team. http://www.accel-team.com/productivity/productivity_02_how.html.

Pryus, M. 2006. Pyramid with Physical Activity. United States Department of Agriculture. www.USDA.gov/nutrition.

Reistad-Long, S. Chow down on eats that tame hunger and reduce anxiety. Yahoo! Health. http://health.yahoo.com/featured/87/8-foods-that-fight-stress/.

Rosch, P. J. The role of stress at work. http://www.ais/stress.org.

Sanborn, Mark. 2004. The Fred Factor: How Passion in Your Work and Life Can Turn the Ordinary into the Extraordinary. New York: Doubleday.

United States Department of Agriculture. Find healthy eating choices. United States Department of Agriculture. http://www.nutrition.gov.

United States Department of Agriculture. Top the pyramid. *ADA Journal* (November 2009): 174:11, 30–36.

US News and World Report. Advances in telecommuting. Central Broadcasting System (CBS), March 21, 2008.

Vedantam, Shankar. 2006. Social isolation growing in U.S., study says. *The Washington Post*. June 23, Nation section. http://www.washingtonpost.com/wp-dyn/content/article/2006/06/22/AR2006062201763.html.

About the Author

Frances (Fran) D. Szabo has a strong business background with more than twenty years in management at Fortune 100 companies and a passion and expertise for learning and change management. She has managed large-scale mergers and developed curriculum for frontline employees through executive employees, including basic skills training for frontline employees and strategic management, and sales and customer service training for executives. She has strong skills converting instructional materials from classroom to distance-learning methods and extensive knowledge of learning management systems. She desires great challenges and is motivated by making a difference in people's lives.

Fran is currently the owner of AdvantEdge, a small business management consulting firm specializing in business learning solutions. Her clients cover a broad range of industries, including hospitality, finance, insurance, manufacturing, education, and health care. This is preceded by a thirty-year career with a blend of roles in operations, management, staff support, and academics.

Fran began working in retail positions and as a seamstress, a dishwasher, a waitress, and a cook while saving money to go to college. Once she graduated with a bachelor's degree in psychology in 1983 from the University of California, Davis, she began working for Marriott International. One of her first lessons learned was to follow her heart, not only her head. She had a love for working with and serving people and still does today. Her family counseled her about making food service management a very brief career as it would not pay very much.

A friend asked her, "How much money do you make working in food service?" Her reply was, "You want to know how much I make? I make a difference. How about you?"

Fran was given several promotions, including one to become general manager as she began studies at the University of San Francisco. She received a master's degree in human resources and organizational development. She continued to take on a variety of roles that crossed between operations and staff positions, including recruiter, business opening swat team leader, human resources manager, area operations manager, training manager, health care new product development manager, training director, and chief learning officer with both Marriott and Sodexo, Inc. She took on many international assignments, giving her experience conducting business throughout North America, England, Scotland, Germany, Austria, France, Italy, India, South Africa, and South Korea. She held professorial roles at the University of Maryland and the University of Delaware from 1989 through 2001.

Fran completed her doctorate in 2004 at Revans University, located in England. She is currently the North American accrediting advisor representing Revans University. She chose to retire from Sodexo in 2006 to pursue more of her ambitions, including opening a business, working with clients in a variety of industries, and writing this book.

Index

All pages numbers in **Bold** refer to References in back of book.

brain
  creative part of, 21
  dopamine and, 80
  linear processing part of, 20
  reaching both sides of, 23
breaks, taking, 40
Brown, Barbara, 4
Buckingham, Marcus, 1, **99**
Bureau of Labor Statistics, 3, **100, 101**

C

cardio activity, 67
career and non-work life, balancing
  about, 63–64
  creating stress-free workplace,
    84–87
  foods that fight stress, 79–80
  keeping optimistic in managing
    stress, 83–84
  "mind like water" thinking,
    87–88
  nutrition, and making healthy
    choices, 68–71
  regular physical activity, 65–68
  relaxation activities, 88–90
  setting boundaries, 64
  stress-related illnesses,
    determinants of, 80–83
  tips for maintaining balance,
    90–91
  USDA recommended food
    consumption (tables), 72–79
Carnes, Ken, 3, 7, **99**
Center for Disease Control (CDC),
  65, 66, **101**
Chavez, Maria, xi–xii
Chicago Tribune, 51, **100**

children
  care of, 33, 40
  home office and areas of, 29
  setting aside time for, 35
  working at home with small, 40
Childress, John R., 1, **99**
Churchard, Claire, 2, **99**
Clinton, Bill, 13
Coffman, Curt, 1, **99**
communication process. *See also*
    behavioral skills
  effective communication skills,
    11–12
  model, 11
communications
  conference call, 42, 43, 51–55
  e-mail, 34, 46–49
  technology reference (table),
    58–59
  video conferencing, 55–59
  voice mail, 49–51
complex projects, working on, 43
cone of silence, creating, 42
conference calls, 42, 43, 51–55
Conrad-Stoppler, M., **99**
Consumers Reports Books, Editors
  of, 34, 86, **100**
contemporary models,
  organizations, 1–2
Cottrell, David, 3, 7, 83, 84, **99**
Covey, Stephen R.
  balancing career with life
    activities, 63, 90
  managing productivity, 45
  physical activity and proper
    nutrition, importance of, 91
  "sharpening the saw," 64
  stereotypes of working, 9
  work habits, 4
  References, **100**
crafting e-mail messages, 46–49